TOP NOTCH
INTERVIEWS

D0950980

Brian Davis

TOP NOTCH INTERVIEWS

Tips, Tricks, and Techniques From the First Call to Getting the Job You Want

CAREER PRESS

Franklin Lakes, NJ

Copyright © 2010 by Brian Davis

All rights reserved under the Pan-American and International Copyright Conventions. This book may not be reproduced, in whole or in part, in any form or by any means electronic or mechanical, including photocopying, recording, or by any information storage and retrieval system now known or hereafter invented, without written permission from the publisher, The Career Press.

TOP NOTCH INTERVIEWS
EDITED BY NICOLE FAHEY
TYPESET BY EILEEN MUNSON
Cover design by Jeff Piasky
Printed in the U.S.A. by Courier

To order this title, please call toll-free 1-800-CAREER-1 (NJ and Canada: 201-848-0310) to order using VISA or MasterCard, or for further information on books from Career Press.

The Career Press, Inc., 3 Tice Road, PO Box 687,
Franklin Lakes, NJ 07417
www.careerpress.com

Library of Congress Cataloging-in-Publication Data
Davis, Brian, 1970-
 Top notch interviews : tips, tricks, and techniques from the first call to getting the job you want / by Brian Davis.
   p. cm.
 Includes bibliographical references and index.
 ISBN 978-1-60163-114-5 – ISBN 978-1-60163-743-7 (ebook) 1. Employment interviewing.
2. Job hunting. I. Title.

 HF5549.5.I6D383 2010
 650.14′ 4--dc22

            2010003396

For Stacy,

Miranda,

and Mitchell

• • • • •

Let your own discretion be your tutor.
Suit the action to the word, the word to the action.

—William Shakespeare,
Hamlet, Prince of Denmark (Hamlet, III, ii)

CONTENTS

• • • • •

Foreword

I have run a successful international recruiting company, interviewed thousands of candidates, read dozens of books on interviewing, and attended numerous seminars on recruiting, interviewing, and career transition. Through all my years of experience in the recruiting industry and leading a global recruitment company, I have yet to find a single source that really teaches candidates how to win interviews. There are countless resources available that teach you how to get an interview or what to do after the interview. However, none of these resources detail what to do during the critical time you spend actually sitting across from the interviewer. There just is not much material out there that addresses this crucial aspect of the hiring process. Therefore, in an effort to assist anyone faced with an upcoming interview, I have decided to impart my years of experience to you with the hopes that you can win interviews and land your dream career.

Every day, thousands of interviews are won and lost. More often than not, they are lost. Once an interview is lost, there is seldom an opportunity to win it back, especially in this competitive marketplace where employers have numerous candidates for every open position. Even if you are the most qualified candidate, have the perfect resume, and possess the right background and career path for a particular opportunity; you may still lose the interview and the job if your interviewing skills are not sharp. As with any skill-based discipline, the more you practice, the better you will perform. The information in this book will teach you the skills required to win interviews.

Think of it this way: What separates the thousands of golfers with a scratch handicap from the few touring professionals?

Answer: Continuous skill refinement and unparalleled focus.

I am not suggesting that you become a professional interviewer, but I do propose that when you enter into a career transition period, you do two things:

- Sharpen your interviewing skills so that you will be in a position to win every interview.

- Make your career transition your number-one priority. No window shopping or testing the market.

I know that many of you will not want to read the entire book, complete the SOAR (pg. 113) worksheet templates, or rehearse your responses. You'd rather just tear out the reference card in the back of the book and quickly scan it the morning of your interview, thinking you have it covered. Believe me, you will not perform as well as if you had read, practiced, rehearsed, and completed all the templates well in advance of your interviews. Remember the reference to the golfers...even if you hit a great shot every now and then, it does not mean that you are ready for the PGA Tour.

Through our global recruiting business, we have helped thousands of candidates reach their career goals by teaching them how to win interviews by using my proven technique—the SOAR Method. I am confident that if you practice and apply the SOAR Method and focus on your career search, you too will win your interviews and reach your career goals faster than you ever imagined.

Thanks! Enjoy the read and be sure to send me your success stories.

• • • • •

Career Transition Preparation

When you are looking for a new career or position, your number-one priority should be your job search. This is the focus we mentioned in the foreword that separated the thousands of scratch golfers from the few we see on television. If you are not focused, your results will be varied at best. I am not so naive as to expect you to put your life completely on hold while you look for a job, but I do challenge you to ask yourself just how serious you really are.

Prioritizing your values and goals is a critical step in your career transition process that will help you identify careers that would be appealing to you. The following categories are guidelines that will help you determine where your career search will take you. Remember, we will not cover in detail the methods you will need to use in order to get to the interviews. However, we will help you make sure that the interviews you choose are ones you can win.

You should begin the process of prioritizing your values and goals by answering the following three questions. Your responses do not have to be any of the ones included in the lists; they are only there to help point you in the right direction. Nor is this exercise a personality profile—it is a tool to help you see just how focused you really are.

What Is Most Important to Me in a Job?

We all have different motivations as to our professional careers. By understanding what really drives your decisions, you can select companies that will allow and help you to achieve your professional goals. For example, if your professional goal is to be the chief financial officer for a global logistics company, and you have very limited international or financial experience, you might want to focus on professional development rather than security.

- Prestige: status in society, public recognition, company name recognition.

- Advancement: opportunity to move up or get promoted.

- Security: job stability, comfort.

- Success: incremental goal achievement, sense of accomplishment.

- Professional Development: formalized program, mentorship.

- Helping Others: helping people, benefiting society.

Professional: _____

Your personal goals and values differ from your professional ones because they are decisions that are centered on the time you will spend away from work. Often, job seekers neglect to include these when they take on a new position or career, only to discover six months later that their personal values cannot be met with their newly undertaken responsibilities. I can tell you countless stories of candidates that indicated they were "Money Motivated," but lacked the work ethic to support their compensation expectations. Know your limits and be honest with yourself.

- Money: salary, benefits, perks.

- Family: spending adequate time with family.

- Commute: limits, stress tolerance, fuel or public transportation costs.

- Leisure: personal time, vacations, activities.

- Travel: amount of time you are willing to be away from home.

Personal: _____

_____

_____

Your work role is how you see yourself functioning in your new career or position. If you know that you cannot take direction and need to freely express your ideas in a non-time sensitive environment, then why would you interview for a Project Manager position? Because it is in the right place for the right salary? Wrong answer. You would only be setting yourself up for confrontation and frustration that would later result in a period on your resume that will be tough to explain in future interviews.

- Variety: doing different things at work or performing similar tasks frequently.

- Independence: freedom to do things your way, on your time.

- Power: authority and influence on what happens.

- Enjoyment: the degree to which you enjoy your job.

- Task-oriented: you need someone else to set your tasks and goals.

Work Role: _____

_____

_____

What Is the Ideal Corporate Culture in Which You Would Thrive?

Over the years, I have seen many definitions of corporate culture, but this one from *dictionary.bnet.com* seems to sum it up best: the combined beliefs, values, ethics, procedures, and atmosphere of an organization. Many job seekers confuse the environment with the culture because of their limited exposure to the office, plant, or people. The environment is a component of the corporate culture, but can often mask the true inner workings and "personality" of a company. We will cover more on culture later, but take time now to jot down your ideas for an ideal culture.

- Atmosphere/environment: friendly and open or stuffy and rigid.

- Teamwork: work together or more individually.

- Competition: big fish in little pond or climb the corporate ladder.

- Work pace: self-directed or deadline-oriented.

- Values based: Are values defined and discussed? Is that important to you?

My Ideal Corporate Culture: _____

_____

_____

How Important Is Geography to Me?

This question is always at the top of my list when talking to candidates. You would be surprised to learn how many candidates have not gone through the exercise of determining their geographical boundaries. These could be cities or regions for those willing to relocate for the right career position. For most, however, the limitations should be a predetermined commutable distance that you know you can tolerate. I have seen countless candidates extend their commutable distance only to become frustrated a few months later once they realize how much time they are spending in the car and away from their family or free-time activities. With the exception of a very few virtual careers, where you want to live will determine where you work, or vice-versa. If you are geographically restricted to a certain area, know that your job search will be harder than someone else who is open to any market. I do not say this to scare you or attempt to force you into opening up your boundaries, but rather to put into perspective the time that it may take you to find your next career. Geographic restrictions are fine—you just need to be sure you account for this in your search.

If you are open and willing to move for a position, be sure that you fully understand the cultural and demographic differences between locations. Also understand that, depending on the industry you are targeting, job opportunities may be centered around industry hubs.

My Location Preferences: _____

_____

_____

_____

• • •

I once had a candidate interview for and secure a position as a distribution manager for a major national retail outlet. The position was located in rural Georgia and the candidate told me that she would gladly move anywhere to join this well respected company. The day of her final interview, I received a call from the hiring manager who said they loved the candidate and would be drafting an offer for delivery the next day. Obviously, at this point I was excited too, as I was about to make a sale. I then remembered that I should call the candidate to let her know about the forthcoming offer. After exchanging pleasantries, I let her know that she won the interview and we were successful in getting an offer presented. Much to my surprise, she politely told me that she would have to pass on this opportunity. When I asked why she said, "Brian, I just can't work in a town that doesn't have a Starbucks!" I could not believe it. I asked her about the company—she loved it; the people—she loved them; the compensation package—more than she was expecting. I even offered to send her Starbucks ground coffee until they put a store in town, but at the end of the day, she just wouldn't budge. So, understand that your geographic limitations may encompass more than just a dot on a map, and be sure to research before getting in too deep with a potential employer.

•

Timeline

When you are ready to interview, you should be ready to start your new position or career very soon thereafter. Very few companies interview more than 90 days in advance of their targeted fill date. If you are relocating, most companies will give you a bit more time than the standard two weeks' notice to start employment, but make sure you have already started the preparations on your end. I have seen numerous accepted offers get rescinded because the candidate could not move out of their house or terminate their lease when they expected. If you're changing jobs locally, be sure to provide notice to your current employer according to the terms in your employee handbook. If you do not have an employee handbook use the unwritten rule of two weeks' notice.

When providing notice to your current employer, simply state, "I have accepted another opportunity and am giving you my two weeks' notice." I also recommend that you present your manager, supervisor, or human resources department with a signed and dated letter of resignation. Prepare this letter at home and only present it once you have officially accepted your new position. Your resignation will spark a conversation and often the employer will want to know where you are going, how much you are getting paid, and why you are leaving. You are under no obligation to provide any of this information, nor are you required to participate in an exit interview. The exit interview is simply a tool companies use to track reasons for resignations and departures, and to prevent them from any future claims of unfair employment practices on their part. When asked if you would be willing to conduct an exit interview, simply state, "No, thanks!"

If you are in any type of outside sales, be ready to have your employer tell you to finish up much sooner than in two weeks. Typically, companies do not like to keep sales representatives in the field when they have already checked out. Most likely, you will conduct a turnover with your manager the same or next day, and be asked to step aside.

It can take anywhere from two days to six months to get the position you want. It all depends on the industry, the level of the position, the location, and the speed in which the company moves you through the process. Just remember that this is a life-changing process, and sometimes a slower process may work in your favor. If for whatever reason you find yourself in a time sensitive situation (you are out of work and your savings account is running low), know that you may have to sacrifice some of your long-term career goals and values in order to meet your more immediate personal financial obligations by taking a position that is not ideal.

Documentation

Being prepared with all the proper documentation is a clear demonstration to your future employer that you are focused on your search, organized, and goal-oriented. It also comes in handy should the potential employer require that you fill out an internal application form as a part of the interview process.

• • •

I once had two candidates interviewing for the same position with the same company. Both candidates emerged through the interview process in neck-and-neck competition for the offer. Candidate A listened to our advice and had the required supporting documentation ready to present upon conclusion of his final interview. Candidate B did not properly plan and exited the interview in a panic, attempting to run around and gather information that could take days or even weeks to assemble in the hopes of getting the offer. Candidate A was presented the offer the next day.

•

Here are some of the items that you should have ready to hand to an interviewer. I also tell all my candidates to scan each of the following and carry them with you to an interview on a flash drive. That way, if you need copies for additional interviewers or the potential employer asks for them in electronic format, you have them with you and do not create an unnecessary delay in the process by sending them later.

IMPORTANT: Do not offer any of the following to the interviewer until asked!

Resume

There are plenty of books dedicated solely to resume preparation, so I will not attempt to cover all resume topics. Rather, I will highlight many of the items that interviewers will focus on when scanning your resume. Your resume is a brief snapshot of your professional career to date, and you should update your resume at least every two years, even if you are happily employed. I recommend this practice because it forces you to document your accomplishments and quantify your results.

Keep in mind that most hiring managers spend less than two minutes reading a resume before conducting an interview. While your resume is a key tool in your career search, you should not spend hours on end preparing it. The tips and samples provided in this book should help you develop a concise, articulate document representative of your past performance and future potential.

Types of Resumes

Ninety-five percent of the readers of this book will use either a chronological or combination resume to document their performance. Here are the four main resume types and where they are most commonly used.

- Chronological—The most common resume format lists your work history first, starting with your most recent position and working backwards. Most human resource professionals prefer this format because it allows them to work backwards and follow your career progression during their line of questioning. This type of resume is most often seen from job-seekers with a strong, solid work history.

- Functional—This type of resume focuses on your skills and experience, rather than on your chronological work history. This format is mostly used when job seekers are either attempting to completely change career fields, hide gaps in their resumes, or if they are reentering the workforce after an extended period of time.

- Combination—This style is often used by more senior executives that want to show both their skill set and their chronological work history. Skills and areas of expertise are listed first and then the work history follows.

- Curriculum Vitae—Commonly referred to as a CV, although I like to call them Euro-Resumes. It is a Latin term that translates to "a running life" or "course of life" that is primarily used in the United States when applying for academic, education, scientific, or research positions. CVs are usually longer documents that list detailed training, publications, awards, honors, and affiliations.

Many of the following items may seem like common sense or as if I am telling you what not to do moreso than what to do. This is because I have received feedback from hundreds of human resource professionals and hiring managers on what they look for and what they do not like to see documented in resumes.

Your resume should be broken down into separate, easy-to-navigate functional areas. Depending on your experience, these functional areas will differ. Please refer to the Sample Resumes at the end of the book for recommendations. All resumes, however, should follow these basic functional areas and rules:

Document Setup

- Templates—Do NOT use a Microsoft Word or Online Template. Many job hunters think that these templates will provide them with a good format for their resume. What they do not realize is that most resumes are first viewed as e-mail attachments and not as printed documents. If one of these templates is used, the tables, lines, and revisions can be seen by the person viewing the document. Start with a blank Word document and build your resume from scratch.

- Header and Footer—Leave these areas of the document blank. Do not add page numbering or insert your contact information into the header or footer. Keep all the content in the main body of the document. As with the templates, most resumes are first viewed as e-mail attachments and the viewer may have their screen set up to hide headers and footers in their view.

- Paper—For printed copies of your resume, use 8.5" x 11" standard white paper. It is recommended that you use a heavy bond or weight for paper copies, but keep it white. Some larger companies scan resumes and white works best. Do not add a scent to your resume and do not add or use paper with pre-printed borders, frames, or lines. Additionally, do not insert your digital picture into the resume. While you should have a professional digital picture available, it does not belong on your resume.

- Font—Use a common font for all text. I recommend Arial, Times New Roman, Veranda, or Garamond. If you use an odd font that is not supported by the viewer's system, your resume may not completely convert, and data will be unreadable to the reviewer. Also, stick with the same font throughout the entire document. Do not use colors. Stick to the standard black. It is acceptable to use bolded, italicized, or underlined text to bring attention to parts of your resume, but avoid going overboard. The font size for everything except your name should be between 9 and 12 point. Your name should stand out in a 14 to 16 point bolded font.

- Margins and Length—I recommend keeping your resume to one page in most circumstances. Some more experienced job seekers can justify a two-page resume, but only if it makes a one page version look too cramped. Start with an Arial 10- or 11-point font and adjust accordingly. Your margins should be set to a half-inch for the top and bottom and between one-half inch and one inch for the left and right. These can also be adjusted to fit the text. Our samples are all set to a half inch for the top, bottom, left, and right. Avoid blank spaces. Never have more than one line of unused space between sections.

Common Resume Format Errors

Here is a list of some of the most common errors and pet peeves from hiring managers and human resource professionals:

- Inconsistent style—Do not list dates differently, use varying font attributes, different margin settings, etc.

- State Abbreviations—Use the standard USPS format (two letters, both capitalized, no period).

- Markup—Make sure you turn off the markup function when editing or revising your resume. If you send it with markup enabled, the reviewer can see all your revisions, when they were made, and who made them.

- Lines & Borders—Remove anything that is not text.

- Document Title—Just use your name, not John_Doe_sales_version_28.

- Periods on Bullets—Do not put periods at the end of bulleted statements. There is no need for them.

- Bullet Style—Do not use imported icons or graphics. Only use standard Word selections.

Contact Information

- Name—I recommend that your contact information be at the top of your resume and centered. Your name should include your nickname if you prefer to be addressed by such (for example, Michael "Chip" Jones). This way, potential interviewers will not question your voicemail greeting should the name not match what is listed on your resume.

- Address—There is an emerging trend among job seekers to only list their city and state to protect their personal information from scammers that search job boards for personal data. This is more than acceptable if you intend on adding your resume to any databases. If you do not plan on submitting it to any job boards, then be sure to list your complete address with unit or apartment number, city, state, and zip code.

- Phone—List either your home or mobile number. You should only list the main number you will use during your career search. Be sure to check you messages daily and return all calls within 24 hours. Make sure your voice message is professional and energetic.

- E-mail—I suggest that you create a separate e-mail account that you will use solely for your career search. There are numerous free services, but I recommend Gmail or Hotmail as they are free, popular, and least likely to be mistyped by the person attempting to contact you. Only list your current work e-mail if your current employer knows you are looking. Your work e-mail is not private and can legally be accessed by your employer, so whatever you send or receive through that account is spotlighting your actions. Lastly, do not have any slang or inappropriate handles in your e-mail address, as it will be viewed as unprofessional by the interviewer. Keep it simple and tied to your name. (jdoe77@isp.com or billsmith12@isp.com)

• • •

Whenever I give this advice, I am reminded of a story about a young sailor who we were attempting to place into a civilian role upon his transition from active duty service in the Navy. We were recruiting for a very specific type of technician to work in the shipyards and the hiring manager was also a former sailor, very patriotic and very proud of his service, so he knew exactly the skill set he needed for the position. Our candidate had the perfect background and lived right in the local area. At first glance, it looked like one of the easiest placements we would ever make. After screening the candidate, our account executive submitted the resume to the hiring manager, but he failed to ask what the weird string of letters in the candidate's e-mail address stood for. Upon receipt of the resume, the hiring manager called us before even interviewing our candidate and asked why we would send him someone that obviously hated the Navy so much. We were baffled until he shared with us what the acronym in his e-mail really stood for—which meant "I hate the Navy." Proper decorum prevents me from spelling it out, but suffice it to say that it stood for less than approving thoughts towards the Navy. The candidate lost a very good opportunity all because he failed to follow this simple rule.

•

Additional Information

- Security Clearance—If you are looking for government or contracting work, it is acceptable to list your clearance if it is active, capable of becoming active, and above secret.

- Professional Experience—Professional experience should be broken down into two distinct segments for each job or position you have held: Position Description and Quantifiable Bullets.

  ⮠ Position Description—Think of this as your two- to three-sentence job description. It should not be written in the third person (common error), nor should it use too much technical or industry jargon. The description should cover your duties and responsibilities, size of your team and/or the budget you led, and to whom you reported.

  ⮠ Quantifiable Bullets—These are the specific individual accomplishments that you (not your team, work group, or unit) achieved during your period with that position or employer. This is where you have to be ready to talk about yourself and clearly demonstrate how you made an impact on a project, business unit, line item expense, sales goal, etc. Nothing adds more validity to a bullet than a number, so be sure to use dollars, percentages, time lines, or anything else you can justify.

When formatting your bullets, keep these guidelines in mind:

- Capitalize the first letter of each bullet.

- Indent slightly from the position description.

- Draw attention to your quantifiable results by using bold or italic fonts on key words.

- Keep your bullets short and no longer than a simple phrase.

- Do not use periods.

Action Words

Accomplished	Founded	Reduced
Achieved	Implemented	Reengineered
Adapted	Improved	Revised
Advanced	Increased	Scheduled
Applied	Introduced	Selected
Attained	Led	Shortened
Awarded	Marketed	Simplified
Constructed	Organized	Solved
Created	Overcame	Spearheaded
Decreased	Projected	Streamlined
Developed	Qualified	Undertook
Earned	Recognized	Enabled
Exceeded	Redesigned	Wrote

- Know what bullet points you listed and be prepared to relay a SOAR story on each.

- Always start your bullets off with an impactful action word to catch the reviewer's attention.

The chart on page 29 lists some great action words to help you develop your Quantifiable Bullets.

Education

I like to list education below work history because interviewers tend to be more critical of education, especially with recent college graduates, and it gives you the opportunity to discuss all your professional accomplishments before discussing your educational history. Recent college graduates should list their part-time jobs and activities first.

- List your school first, then degree type and major if it correlates to the position, and then the graduation year.

- You only need to list the graduation year, not all years attended. This is because anything more than four years could open the door for the interviewer to question you as to why it took you longer than average to graduate.

- Always list your highest degree first.

- There is no need to list your high school, unless that is the highest level attained.

- You do not need to list your Associates Degree if you have a four-year degree.

- List any clubs, organizations, or teams of which you were a member. If you held a leadership position within the group, be sure to list it as well.

Examples:

- President, XYZ Fraternity

- Defensive Captain, Varsity Football

If you personally financed any or all of your education, or if you were awarded any scholarship funds, be sure to list them.

Examples:

- Self financed 40 percent of costs working weekends and evenings

- Awarded XYZ scholarship for academic excellence

Only list your GPA if it is a 3.0 or better. Do not list your Major GPA unless your overall is above 3.0. This looks like a feeble attempt to show you were smart and focused, but only in areas that interested you.

List any additional significant accomplishments.

Examples:

- Volunteer tutor for Math Department

- Graduated ahead of schedule in less than four years

What NOT to put on your resume

I highly discourage listing any information on your resume that is confidential or that would otherwise be excluded for an interview due to protective legal issues. Some of the items in this list are not allowed for discussion during an interview unless brought up or disclosed by the candidate. Do not open a can of worms by including it on your resume.

- Age or Date of Birth—While most recruiters or interviewers will make some assessment of your age based on your work history and the dates and graduation years, they are not allowed to ask your age.

- Spouse's and Children's Names and Ages—I often see these listed by mothers reentering the workforce and trying to justify what they have been doing for the past 18 years.

- Religious or Political Affiliations—This is about the fastest way to get your resume rejected that I can think of. If you list that you are a card-carrying member of the Republican Party, you only have a 50/50 chance that the person reviewing your resume has the same political views. If not, then you get moved to the bottom of the stack.

- Desired Salary—Why on earth anyone would list this on a resume is beyond my ability to comprehend. In doing so you could be limiting yourself in one of two ways. First, you might be underselling your skills, talents, and experiences and put yourself in a position when you get the job but at a lower rate than the employer had originally intended to pay. Second, you might price yourself out of a position before ever even interviewing. The employer may get intimidated by your salary demand and simply move on to other candidates with lower expectations. If the application process specifically asks for a salary history, then provide one on a separate document. We will discuss salary negotiation later on, but for now just remember to leave this off your resume.

- Height/Weight and Health Status—Employers are prohibited from asking any of this data, so why offer it up? Employers are legally restricted to providing the physical requirements of the position and asking if you can meet them. If you are really proud of yourself and want to demonstrate that you are physically fit, then include a bullet at the bottom of your resume that demonstrates this.

Examples:

➲ Avid runner and tri-athlete

➲ Enjoys rock-climbing, surfing, and other outdoor activities

- Race—many online application portals will include a voluntary OFCCP (Office of Federal Contract Compliance Programs) section that includes questions regarding your sex and ethnic origin. None of these are required, and it is entirely up to you if you choose to participate.

- Social Security Number—When the time is right and the employer needs to run a background check before making you an offer, they will have you sign a release. Then and only then should you provide your SSN. Especially in today's digital world, the less you have your SSN floating around in cyberspace, the better.

- Date of Availability—All employers assume that if you supplied them a resume, either directly or through a recruiter, that you are ready to start work in a reasonable period of time (typically two days to one month).

- Objective Statement—In all my years of recruiting, I have never seen an objective statement help a candidate. Unless the objective is 100 percent in line with the company culture, position descriptions, the interviewer's personal style, and position requirements, the interviewer will only find reasons why you would not fit based on this wonderfully scripted, generic, catch-all phrase. Leave it out!

- References Available Upon Request—It is understood by all interviewers and hiring managers that you will provide these upon request.

- Company Confidential—This may be acceptable for resumes posted online, but by the time you are in an interview, you should list all employers.

- Pictures—All interviewers do place a weight on "Impact Presence" but let that sell itself in person, not on your resume. Some job seekers think that including a picture of themselves will help them land an interview. If that is the case, then the future employer is looking at you for all the wrong reasons and not making a business decision based on your skills and experiences.

  You might also be limiting yourself by including your picture, as the person reviewing the resume may have a cultural bias that is represented in your picture. While it is illegal for them to eliminate you because of these reasons, it does happen so don't give them the opportunity. It is much harder to prove a discrimination case from a resume submission than from a personal interview.

Resume Writing Services

As you start to distribute and post your resume, you will come across numerous businesses offering resume preparation or review services. Depending on your level of experience, your targeted position, and your intended resume marketing efforts; these services could be a benefit or a complete waste of your hard-earned money.

If you really do not know where to start in formulating a resume, or if your resume is not getting you the interviews your peers are getting, then you should consider these services. Here are a few tips for selecting a resume writing service provider:

- Cost—Never spend more that 1 percent of what you expect to earn annually on your resume preparation.

Example: Your annual salary is about $60,000. You should not spend more than $600 in resume preparation. Most services are already priced in this range, so you will not have to worry about it. But beware, if you come across a company that tries to sell you a package that is more than 1 percent, move on to another service. Remember to keep your receipts from your transactions, as resume preparation is a tax deductible expense.

- Industry—By doing a simple Internet search, you are bound to find resume writing experts that specialize in your industry or field. Use them! They know the latest trends and keywords used by recruiters when searching for candidates. At a minimum, ask to see sample resumes from your industry that the resume writer has recently produced. Also ask for references and referrals.

- Revisions—Ask how many revisions you get. The initial product might not meet your expectations and you want the ability to ask for more work. A resume writer, no matter how good, will never get everything correct on the first attempt.

- Format—Some resume writers will only deliver their finished work to you in an uneditable format like a .pdf file. These are no good to you, as you cannot edit them. This is merely a trick used to get you to come back to them for additional services or revisions that end up costing you more money. Legitimate resume preparation services deliver your products in editable files such as Microsoft Word files.

- Free Resume Reviews—Many popular job boards now offer "Free Resume Reviews" to job seekers that register on their site. Before you dive in, you should understand what is really transpiring. More often than not, the "Free Resume Review" is being outsourced to another party, typically an individual that has a contractual relationship with the job board that does not get paid unless you agree to revise your resume with them. The job board then gets a cut of the transaction for providing the sales lead. The job board gets paid, the resume writer gets paid, and you get told how horrible your resume is and that you will never get interviews unless you use their service.

I recently submitted a resume for a "Free Review" that I drafted for a candidate to a major job board. In return, I got back an e-mail that to me looked like a fill-in-the-blank template that pointed out five reasons why my resume would never get me the interviews I was after. I then purchased the resume writing package for a complete overhaul. In my opinion, the product I got back was far inferior to the one originally submitted. Regardless, I then submitted the very same newly revised resume back under a different name and account and guess what? I received the same standard message stating the five reasons why I needed a revision package. This is not the case with all resume writing service providers, but it does happen.

Mid- to Senior-Level Executives: If you fall into this category, then you should definitely consult with a professional resume preparation service provider because you have probably seen what you think are some pretty sharp resumes come across your desk over the years and have kept a file of the good ones to use as a guideline. The problem is that they might look good to you, but not to a C-level recruiter. I have seen just about every type and format for executive resumes, but none compare to the products produced by the team at www.helpmesellme.com. Their work is not cheap, but it does fall into my 1 percent rule.

Finalizing Your Resume

- Spell/Grammar check—Make sure you run it every time you update or change your resume. We all make typos, and it is hard to catch our own with the naked eye because our mind is already pre-programmed as to what we intended to type. Additionally, I strongly suggest that you have someone that has excellent language and grammar skills proofread your resume.

- No gaps—If you have periods of unemployment, extended leave, or travel, be sure to list them. Interviewers become suspicious when they see gaps and will exploit them. Better to be honest up front and avoid the negative questions.

- References—References should not be an afterthought that you scramble to collect at the last minute. Rather, you should have them prepared before you ever submit your resume or agree to an interview. You should also call any references that you list and ask for their permission to list them as a personal or professional reference. All your references should be on a separate document from your resume. Have at least three personal and three professional references all on the same page.

  What to include with each reference cited:

  ➲ Name

  ➲ Title/position

  ➲ Company or relationship

  ➲ Contact information

  ➲ Phone

  ➲ E-mail

  ➲ Quote or excerpt from performance evaluation

➲ Letter of recommendation (if provided) on a separate document

- Personal References—Non-family friends that can speak to your character. It is okay to list former business associates here as long as they were not in your direct line of management (either they supervised you or you supervised them). It is also acceptable to list former clients here, as they will confirm your passion and ability to follow through.

  - Former teachers

  - Community leaders

  - Church leaders

- Professional References—Current and former supervisors, managers, or board members. Do not list professional references that have a lower position or title than the targeted position you are seeking. In other words, do not list an entry-level engineer as a reference if you are attempting to secure a VP of Engineering position.

- Samples—In the Appendix, there are sample resumes and a sample reference sheet for you to see how they are laid out and how the content is presented.

Cover Letters

You should always include a cover letter whenever you send out your resume, either electronically or via mail. Because most resumes are now sent through job boards or by email, the more traditional cover letter document is less popular. Regardless of format, you should understand the different types of cover letters and the content you should include in each.

Types of Cover Letters

Depending on who you are sending your resume to and the circumstances, your content will vary slightly. All will follow the following content outline, but the tone and wording for each type will vary slightly.

- Application—This is the most common type of cover letter. It is intended for a specific job opening or published position. You should make reference to how your skills directly relate to the job requirements, and position your experiences to match the published description. This style should always include a line similar to one of the following examples.

  "Please accept my resume in consideration for the _____ position."

  "Please accept my resume in consideration for the position of _____."

  "I am applying for the advertised position of _____."

- Inquiry—A slight variation to the Application style, the inquiry cover letter should address your interest in the company first and then any open positions that meet your experience and skill set. This is the format you should use if sending a "blind" submission. While I do not endorse mass mailings or sendouts for your resume and cover letter, you should use this style if you insist on the mass-mail approach. Some typical inquiry statements include…

  "Please accept my resume for any open positions that match my skill set."

  "I would like to be considered for any available opportunities within your company."

- Networking—A new trend in cover letters is to distribute your resume to your business and social network to seek access to their extended network and advice in your search. This style should indicate why you are on the market and list what type of opportunities you are looking for in your next career move. You should also let the recipients know whether or not it is acceptable for them to forward your resume without your knowledge to their connections. Some key phrases to include in a networking cover letter are:

  "I am currently exploring new career opportunities and would appreciate the additional exposure of my resume to your extended network."

  "Please feel free to forward my resume to members of your network who you think might benefit from my experiences."

Your cover letter should be concise and have a well structured format. In almost all circumstances, it should be limited to one page. With the limit on space, your cover letter should follow the four-paragraph format for maximum impact.

Paragraph 1: Introduction

Use the introduction to state who you are and why you are sending your information. This is also the proper location to get specific regarding the type of cover letter you are sending. When you state what you are after, be sure you include something that catches the reader's attention through a benefit to him or the company. This will help you stand out from the thousands of other cover letters and get that extra minute of the reader's time to review your resume.

Typical Introduction Statement:

"I am applying for the outside sales representative position you have posted on your website."

Benefit-Focused Introduction Statement:

"I have a track record of exceeding sales goals in every position held, resulting in increased sales and profits for my employers. I would welcome the opportunity to discuss exactly how I can deliver the same type of results in the outside sales representative position you have advertised on your website."

Paragraph 2: Selling Points

In this section, you will provide three to four bullets that show more detail about your career experiences, educational qualifications, and specific accomplishments. All of the bullets should be benefit-focused to the employer just like your introduction statement. If you do not have a long list of accomplishments (if you are just starting your career), you can add more detail to your introduction statement or focus on your educational qualifications. The focus of your selling points should be achievement, awards, and accomplishments and not job description, duties, or responsibilities. Start each benefit-focused selling point off with an action word to catch the reader's attention. If you are attempting to gain entry into a new industry and lack specific skills listed in the job posting or description, then highlight your transferable skills.

Examples of Benefit-Focused Selling Points:

- Quantitative—Produces return on investment for company by conducting easy to understand cost benefit analysis and forecasting models. Expert in developing, reading, and interpreting income statements, line item expenses, and other financial reports used to reduce expenses and increase efficiencies.

- Communications—Adept at one-on-one discussions and comfortable presenting to large groups in multiple settings, resulting in improved communications across departments and increasing employee satisfaction.

- Sales Ability—Development of new and existing client base in a business-to-business environment across numerous product lines translates into immediate results for company's bottom line.

- Sales Management—Complete grasp of sales cycle to include prospecting, presentations, pipeline development, closing, and fulfillment, resulting in ability to coach, train, and develop sales superstars for the company.

- Leadership—Visionary and compassionate leader of people who generates buy in and builds trust in the company's mission and goals.

Paragraph 3: Correlation

In this section, you tie in your skills and experiences to the position description and the company. You should relay why you think you would be a fit for the opportunity or the corporate culture of the company. There is no need to demonstrate your knowledge of the company by restating their vision, mission, or any other data published on their Website. It should be apparent in your correlation statement that you have done your research on the position and the company.

Examples of Benefit-Focused Correlation Statements:

- Product-Based Sales Representative: "I believe that my sales skills, work ethic, and demonstrated record of exceeding goals would make me a perfect fit for your Account Manager opportunity. By applying my expert knowledge of the sales process to your quality products,

I can guarantee success in new business development and increase sales to the existing client base."

- Client Relationship Manager: "As a Client Advisor for your company, my enthusiasm, analytical skills, organizational abilities, and natural tendency to develop relationships will make an immediate positive contribution towards client relations. I understand the position calls for individual and team contributions; I am equally comfortable working independently and collaboratively to reach company objectives. I am also open to a high level of travel to meet with clients in person to further the overall relationship."

Paragraph 4: Closing/Call to Action

The final paragraph of your cover letter should be a positive statement that exudes confidence and calls the reader to action. In this statement, you must ask for the opportunity to meet in person or interview. You should also inform the reader of your intentions to follow up until you hear back from them regarding your status.

- Typical (Passive) Closing Statement: "Thank you for your time. I hope to hear from you soon and be selected for an interview."

- Positive (Pro-Active) Closing Statement: "I am confident that, given the opportunity, I will make an impression on your team. I am eager to interview for this opportunity and can schedule an appointment at your earliest convenience. Should I not hear from you by the end of the week, I will call your office to schedule an appointment."

Cover Letter Pitfalls

Here are a few of the most common mistakes that job seekers make when composing cover letters.

- Generic Addressee—If you send out a cover letter addressed to "Hiring Manager," "Dear Sir or Ma'am," or even the dreaded "To Whom It May Concern," you might as well throw your resume in the trash—it will get equal exposure there. Generic addressee cover letters tell the employer that you are not focused enough on the company to spend a few moments of research to find out the name of the person that will be reviewing the documents. Most job postings and online advertisements will tell you how to address your cover letter. If you are working with a recruiter, he or she will provide you the information or act as your cover letter when he or she submits your resume to the employer. If you cannot find out the correct person to send it to through your own research efforts, simply call the company and ask the receptionist, "To whom should I address my cover letter and resume?"

- Restating Your Resume—Some job seekers are so proud of their resumes that they feel the need to copy and paste pieces of it into their cover letter. They are two separate documents with different purposes, so do not intermingle the contents. This should not be a problem if you follow the four paragraph outline.

- Stating Your Goals—It is great to have documented personal goals, but the cover letter is no place for them. Employers do not care what your personal goals are. Rather, they care about how you can benefit their company.

- List of References—Unless the published job description specifically asks for a list of references to be included in the cover letter, attach them as a separate document using the format in the Appendix. Most employers will not spend the time or incur the expense of checking references until much later in the interview process once they have either selected a candidate or have a short list of possible candidates.

- No Contact Information—While you should never send your cover letter without a resume and your resume should always include your contact information; do not assume that the employer will keep both documents together. Just to be safe, include your full name, address, e-mail, and phone number. Most professional business letters include this information just below your signature block.

- No Signature—A cover letter is only personal when you sign it. Use a standard ink pen and a neat, legible signature. If you're sending it digitally, include your full name and phone number.

- Desperation—Cover letters should never sound like you really need the job. You might, but the employer does not care. They want to find people that can add value to their team, not satisfy your personal needs or desires. Avoid phrases like "...can start immediately," or "recently laid off."

- Proofread—Use the spell-check on your computer and have someone you trust proofread your cover letter. It is always best to have another person read what you type before sending out to a potential employer.

Military & Educational Records

If you are transitioning from active duty, you will also need copies of all your pertinent military records. Likewise, if you have ever served in the military, it is a good idea to have a copy of your discharge papers in case they are asked for in a background check.

- DD-214 Form—This official document is the government's Report of Separation and is the most important form all veterans should carry. The DD-214 contains information normally needed to verify military service for benefits, retirement, employment, and membership in veterans' organizations. There are numerous resources on the Internet that will charge you to get a copy of your records, but you can get a free certified copy by visiting *www.archives.gov/veterans/evetrecs/index.html*.

- Military Evaluations—Depending on your branch of service and your rank, you will have had some type of evaluation written on your performance periodically (Fitness Reports, Officer Qualification Records, Officer Performance Report, Basic Training Records, Basic Individual Records). Some employers will ask for these, especially if you are transitioning directly from active duty to the civilian sector, and you should have them ready to present.

- Military Commendations—The military likes to present certificates, ribbons, and medals for performance. If you have ever been awarded any individual awards, then you should have a copy of the commendation ready to share with the interviewer, if asked. Do not include obligatory awards (like the National Defense Service medal) or unit commendations (like the Meritorious Unit Commendation), as they do not translate into any specific contributions you made to an event or occurrence. If the interviewer really understands the military awards system, the will know where to see all your awards on the DD-214.

- Diplomas—Always have a copy of your highest level diploma earned on your flash drive and ready to present at any interview. If you have a GED as your highest, then use that.

- Transcripts—Most colleges and universities will provide you with certified copies of your transcripts for a small fee from the Registrar's office. Have these scanned and on your flash drive. Keep your sealed originals in a safe place in case you need them in the future.

Digital Pictures

While digital pictures do not belong on resumes, it is a really good idea to have a clean, professional digital picture on a flash drive during your interview process. While it is highly unlikely that an interviewer will ever ask for a digital picture, you may be asked for one if you happen to be working with a recruiter or placement agency over the phone. No recruiter will ever admit to this fairly common practice, but by asking for a digital picture they are able to determine your impact presence before submitting you to a client.

If you are not comfortable with providing a picture, then just tell the recruiter or interviewer you will be more than happy to provide a digital picture for your employment records once you are hired.

If you do decide to carry a digital image on your flash drive with you, keep these guidelines in mind:

- Style—The best pose is a traditional head and shoulders shot. If you go to any professional studio and tell them you need a business head and shoulders portrait, they will know what you mean. If you are doing it yourself and need a reference, just Google "business portrait" and take a look at the image results.

- Size—You don't need a billboard-sized 12-megapixel image. The bigger the file is, the more space it takes and the harder it is to e-mail. I recommend a 1–2 megapixel image compressed to fit into a 3" x 5" size.

- Dress—Professional dress is preferred, but a sport coat without a tie for men and business casual for women is also acceptable.

- Background—A studio professional backdrop (blue background) is optimal, but if you do it yourself, just use a plain white wall for your backdrop.

- Just You—As proud as we all are of our families and pets, there really is no place for them in your professional business portrait.

Application Forms

I know you are proud of your resume and you spent countless hours fine-tuning it just for this one interview. But be warned—you may still need to fill out an application form when you arrive if that is the policy of the company you are interviewing with. Many larger companies require this practice to keep in compliance with Equal Employment Opportunity Commission (EEOC) requirements. Some companies also use this as a screening mechanism to see how well you interact with the receptionist.

If the application has a work history section do not write in "See Resume" in the space provided. Get there early, take your time, and use your resume as a guide when filling out the application.

If the application asks for a desired rate or salary and you are not sure what the position you are interviewing for is compensated, simply write "commensurate with experiences." This will leave the door open for a negotiation after you have won the interview.

Online Applications

Most big companies have made the move to a paperless application process and will have you complete an online application before you come in for an interview or complete it onsite before they meet with you. Most will allow you to upload your resume and then parse out the data into the appropriate fields. However, some require manual input. If this is the case, just print out a copy of your resume to use as a guide and enter the data in all the required fields. Even if you have completed an online application, bring a hard copy of your resume with you when you meet in person.

Sales Brag Books

If you are a sales representative or would like to be one, then you really should have a Brag Book. The function of the Brag Book is to substantiate the bullet points and accomplishments you have listed on your resume. Think of it as the documented proof of your achievements. If you have been building your book all along, then you probably already know all about what to include and how to use it. If you are just now assembling your Brag Book, then use this as your checklist for success. If you are missing any of the data that you wish you kept, then call your old employer and ask for a historical file with old copies that you might use. If you do include copies of contracts be sure you have approval to use them from your current employer and that you are within the boundaries of your non-compete or employment agreement.

What to Include

I have seen some crazy things in Brag Books through the years, but here is a list of the best items to include:

- Sales Awards—If you received a certificate for a monthly, quarterly, or annual achievement, then put it in the book. (Pictures of you on stage receiving a plaque or commission check are also appropriate.) If you have several monthly awards, then put them all in. The thicker the book, the better.

- Sales Rankings—Rankings are different from awards in that they show where you stacked up against your peers. Most sales organizations publish some type of report that shows your position relative to the pack. If you are in the top third or better, then highlight your name and throw it in the book.

- Signed Contracts—If you have copies of contracts you sold, then by all means, add them to your book. The more recognizable the client, the better the impact.

- Recognition Events—Sales reward events come in many different names, such as President's Club, Ionosphere, Winners Circle, and Platinum Club. If you received an invitation, or if there was a program with your name listed as a member, then add it to your book.

- Notes from Sales Manager or Executives—Some sales managers or bosses have VIP cards and use them as motivational tools or thank-you notes. If you have any congratulating you on closing a sale or winning a contest, it should go in the book.

- Quotes or Notes from Clients—One sales rep I interviewed had asked all contacts she closed with her previous employer to write a hand-written note on their company letterhead about her service throughout the sales cycle and why they selected her above all her competitors. She had dozens of letters and a story to relay on every single one. Talk about passion—she had it!

- Goals—We all know that sales reps like to proclaim that are all money motivated, so why not show it in your book? One sales rep showed me his book that had a tabbed section for his goals that included plans for his dream house and a picture of the boat he wanted to buy.

- Background and Traffic Check—While most companies will use their own service before presenting an offer, you can alleviate any concerns they might have by providing them with your criminal background and traffic record (both clean, I hope) in your book. There are numerous sources available on the Internet that will allow you to run a criminal background or traffic check on yourself for a small fee (usually around $20). When running a criminal background check, select the county and state of the potential employer and the county and state of your address of record, as that is where the will most likely check. A clean report will show "no history" or "no entries found."

How to Put It Together

I have seen all kinds of Brag Books, from spiral bound materials, to binders, to old fashioned black and white copies held together by a single staple. I strongly recommend that you build yours with either a spiral binding with a nice cover or use a binder with sheet protectors for each insert. You can easily create copies at Kinko's and have one ready to leave with the interviewer. Binders are more expensive, but do look nice. So, have one binder that you keep and have copies of all the contents in the back that you can leave after you have walked your interviewer through your presentation deck. If you have had several positions or worked with several companies, then you might want to invest in some color coded tabs to separate each position for easy reference.

- When to use it—Good sales reps will work a presentation of their Brag Books into the interview as a normal part of the conversation. If you brought it but were not able to share it during the interview, then simply ask the interviewer if he or she would like to see a record of your accomplishments. Have your book presentation rehearsed and be able to go cover to cover in less than five minutes without interruption. You want the interviewer to stop you along the way and ask questions so you can relay a SOAR story for each of the items in your book.

- Work Samples—Similar in composition to a Brag Book would be a work sample portfolio for individuals in the graphic arts, media, architecture, or related fields. It should demonstrate work product you contributed to or created.

Industry Knowledge

Most companies expect their leaders and key players to be well-read with respect to current trends. If you have a specific industry in mind for your career search, you should focus your readings and research on that particular segment.

Organizations and Associations

Most industries have some type of governing body or third-party professional trade organization. If you want to separate yourself from other candidates, then join and assume an active role by contributing content or chairing a committee. While most candidates trade publications, join industry e-mail news groups and blogs, and become a member in at least one professional trade organization.

Reading List

When preparing your reading list, try to focus on a mixture of the following. Obviously you should start within your targeted industry, but diversity shows depth.

- Self-Development Books—Interviewers like to hear that you have a plan for self-improvement and aren't afraid to talk about it.

- Business Periodicals—Some of the most popular business magazines are the best method to keep up with the latest trends and topics.

- Sales Books—No matter what type of position you are interviewing for, a sales book will help. We all sell something every day—products, services, ideas, concepts, etc.

- Process Improvement/Quality Books—These topics relating to how to improve processes and procedures in the workplace will demonstrate your commitment to efficiency and pride in your work.

- Customer Satisfaction Books—Not only do these topics teach you how to better interact with customers, they can also teach you a few things on how to play nice with your fellow employees.

Do not share with interviewers that the last three books you have read have all been on how to interview, or some obscure topic that has no bearing on the business or industry. Rather, demonstrate your desire to join their team by sharing with them the titles that relate to what you will be doing on a daily basis.

• • •

I had a hiring manager call me after interviewing one of my candidates to give me feedback. He started off by saying that he would not be moving the candidate forward in the process. I thought, "Oh well, can't win them all, but at least I can get some good feedback to share with the candidate." The hiring manager said he presented himself well, was very articulate, smart, and had developmental potential. "Then why the heck didn't you hire him?" I asked. "Because he is not doing anything personally to develop himself professionally," he replied. Wow, what a great statement! When I inquired as to how the hiring manager came to that conclusion, he told me that he gave the candidate several opportunities to convey what he had read recently, but all he kept getting in response was, "I am addicted to science fiction books. I can't put them down. I read two to three a week." So you can see why the hiring manager was less than eager to move this candidate along.

•

Financial Research

If the company you are interviewing with is publically traded, then all the information you could possibly want will be filed with the appropriate agency and free to access. You should read the annual report and get a basic understanding of the company's financial position as best you can. We aren't all CFOs, so some of it might be a bit confusing. If the company is privately held, try to gain as much information from the Internet as possible.

A final word of caution for company or industry research: Do not place an ounce of value in anything that a former employee has to tell you unless you absolutely trust the source. Most Websites that offer insider information are typically full of disgruntled former employees that have an ax to grind.

Working With Recruiters

If you had a $100,000 income tax problem, would you attempt to deal with it without the help of a CPA? If you had a $100,000 legal question, would you deal with it without the help of an attorney? Of course not! Then why on earth would you try to enter into a $100,000-career-level decision on your own? Realtors, attorneys, and CPAs all have a cost associated with their services. When dealing with a recruiter, you have zero cost and absolutely no downside risk. It would be foolish to consider a job or career search that does not include utilizing at least one professional recruiter.

Contrary to some people's beliefs, recruiters do not take a cut from your salary. Companies have line item expenses in their budgets set aside for recruiting fees. To better understand this, it helps to understand the types of recruiters you might run across.

Contingency

These are recruiters that only get paid by the employer upon a successful hire. Contingency recruiters typically have multiple job openings with multiple clients all at the same time. The majority of recruiters that will contact you fall into this category.

Retained

These recruiters are given some or all of the fee for their services up front in order to allow them to focus on a specific search for a position. Executive and C-Level positions, which are harder to fill, typically involve a retained search.

Contract

Here, the recruiters work solely for a particular company for a period of time to help fill their openings. This usually occurs when a company has numerous openings or is going through an expansion.

Why Use a Recruiter?

If you are still not convinced of the value of a professional recruiter, here are more reasons to use one:

Network

Most good recruiters do not have to cold call to find jobs. They are presented with them from within their network. Many of the positions are never presented to the public at large or posted on job boards so they are what recruiters refer to as hidden opportunities.

Access

Recruiters work directly with the hiring managers and have access to their schedules for setting up interviews. They understand the interview process and all the players involved that you might otherwise never fully realize.

Inside Scoop

Often, the recruiter can provide you with information regarding the company culture, the work environment, and the backgrounds of the people with whom you will be interviewing. They will also help prepare you for each interview by coaching you on individual styles, likes, and dislikes.

Top of the Stack

Because of the relationships recruiters have with their clients and the way in which they present you as a candidate, your resume will be viewed and your interview will be scheduled sooner than all the other candidates from the job-seeker population at large.

Market Value

Your recruiter can help you determine your true market value in regards to compensation. Recruiters spend their entire existence dealing with open positions and compensation packages, so they know what the market is calling for and how much employers are willing to pay to get it.

Resources

Recruiters have tools available to them that you do not. Most employers today use some type of applicant tracking system and many also have vendor management systems to keep track of their recruiters as well. Your recruiter may have the ability to track your status and view feedback on your progress throughout the interview process.

Time Management

When you are fully engaged in the interview process, your schedule can become quite hectic. You could find yourself in a position in which your availability for interviews with different potential employers might conflict. In these situations, your recruiter can run interference for you and set the employer's expectations as to your availability so you don't have to.

Competition (Candidates)

Your recruiter should tell you who you are up against and what you need to do to better position yourself as the top candidate. The candidates you are up against could be from the same recruiter, another recruiter, the general job-seeker pool, or internal candidates already employed at the company.

Competition (Employers)

Recruiters have the skill required to pull off what is known as the hot candidate tactic. By informing the employer that you are interviewing with other companies and are in high demand, they create a sense of urgency that if you tried to pull off on your own might seem cocky or disingenuous.

Negotiations

Recruiters deal with compensation negotiations every day; you might do it five times in your life. Use the recruiter to act as your agent (like a professional athlete), and you will end up with the best possible deal. It also allows you to start fresh without any animosity between you and your new boss if you just went through a back and forth haggle over money.

Connection

Many business professionals rely on the recruiter who placed them to help staff their openings in their new role. A good recruiter is a go-to connection, whether you are looking for a new position for yourself or for your team.

The recruiting industry is unregulated and, like many industries, has its share of individuals who skirt the ethics line to make a sale. These are the recruiters who view candidates or job seekers merely as a means to justify their end. Your good judge of character will tell you if you are dealing with an unethical recruiter, but just in case, use the following list to help limit your exposure to a recruiter that operates outside good business practices.

What to Look for When Selecting a Recruiter or Firm

Exclusivity

Any recruiter that asks you to sign an exclusivity agreement is bad news. We live in a free market society, so why should you limit your chances to the abilities of just one resource? The only exception to this rule would be if you are a senior level executive with a Fortune 500 company looking for a C-Level position with a base compensation well above 250K per year. Because that eliminates a good majority of the workforce, just remember—exclusivity equals gross limitations on probability of success.

Secrets

If your recruiter wants to submit your resume to a company, but does not tell you the name of the company, run away! Now, understand that during the initial brief where the recruiter wants to gauge your interest level on a position, he or she might not give away the company name. This is a fairly common practice any recruiter might use to test your interest level while protecting his or her client list. The recruiter also does this to prevent you from going directly to the company and submitting your resume through the company website and cutting him or her out of the deal. As previously mentioned, the good recruiters will have relationships in place that you want to use, so do not try this tactic yourself thinking you can do it without the recruiter. Allow the recruiter to give you the pitch, but make sure that he or she always gives you the company name at the end.

No Blind Submissions

This tactic often goes hand-in-hand with the secrets topic. Some companies that deal with numerous recruiting vendors have a "first-in" policy, which refers to the recruiter that submits a resume though their system first. That recruiter gets the credit for the candidate. Because of this, some recruiters submit resumes without ever speaking to the job seekers in hopes they will be a fit and eventually get hired. Whenever you deal with a recruiter, be sure you state that you do not want to be submitted to any positions without giving your approval first.

• • •

I once had a candidate who was in high demand for several medical device sales positions. He had great experience and was very sharp, but he really wanted to stay in Salt Lake City, so he was being selective with his opportunities. I told him to sit tight and whenever I had something in his area, I would call and brief him on it to see if he was interested. About a week later, I received a call from a client in the medical device industry who was looking for a representative to cover Utah, Colorado, and Nevada and that the candidate could live anywhere in the territory. I told him I had his perfect candidate, but needed to circle back with him to see if he was still on the market before I sent him his resume and profile. The client was thrilled to hear it because I had already placed his top three reps and he knew that I delivered talent when needed. I immediately hung up and called my candidate, but got his voicemail. I left him a message telling him to call me ASAP, as I had found the position he had been waiting for. He called me back that same evening and was ecstatic to interview for the opportunity. I submitted his resume later that evening to the client. The next morning,

I awoke to an e-mail from the client informing me that he had already been sent that candidate's resume the day before from another recruiting company and therefore could not accept it from me. I immediately called the candidate to ask why he had not told me about this during our conversation. The candidate was flabbergasted and said he had not spoken to any other recruiters since posting his resume online. I immediately knew that Recruiter X had beaten me to the punch with a blind submission, but I was not going to take it lying down. I called the client and explained what had happened. After he verified with the candidate, he agreed that the credit belonged to me. The other recruiting company was dropped from my client's vendor list and is now out of business.

•

Questions to Ask a Recruiter When First Contacted

If you are still unsure as to how to interact with recruiters when they call, use these simple questions to start your dialog. Then use your judgment to see if they are likeable and have access to the types of positions you are interested in.

How long have you been recruiting?

Obviously we all would prefer working with someone that has been in recruiting for years, but it is okay if the recruiter is new to the industry. Just keep it in mind if the process with them seems to be slow. Your proactive communications will help drive the process.

Have you ever placed candidates with this client before?

If Yes:

- How many?

- What is your retention rate?

- Into what other positions/departments?

If No:

- How many other candidates have you submitted so far?

- Have you had any actual interviews take place yet?

- How long have you been working with this company on this position?

What is the position of your contact within the company?

- Internal Company Recruiter—Most likely a longer process, as they are screeners and have no hiring authority.

- Hiring Manager/Talent Acquisition or Development—Tend to move faster and have authority to schedule and hire.

Are you submitting any other candidates to this position?

It is not a bad thing if they are, but you just want to gauge where you stand.

Other Topics When Dealing With Recruiters

Resume

If your recruiter wants to change your resume, make sure you get a copy back and check it for accuracy before it ever goes to a client. I have seen candidates get dropped from the process because their resume was altered by a recruiter without their knowledge.

Track Contacts

If you are serious about your job search, you will have more than one recruiter representing your interests. I recommend you use a spreadsheet to keep track of each recruiter and the jobs in which you are engaged. It should include the recruiter's contact information, each job, each potential employer's contact information, and notes regarding where you are in the process with each. Keep this spreadsheet with you at all times and update daily.

Keep All Informed

There is no need to hold your cards close to your chest. You are much better off letting each recruiter know that you have other opportunities through other recruiters. You do not necessarily have to tell them the specifics of your other opportunities, but you should let them know what they are competing against. Your recruiters will be better positioned to negotiate on your behalf if they know the full playing field and they can also speed up the process if there is competition.

Call Off the Dogs

Once you accept a new position, just let your other recruiters know so they can professionally remove you from the process with the other positions for which you were interviewing. They will thank you and remember your professionalism should you ever need their services again.

Job Boards

You cannot discuss career transition preparation without mentioning job boards. The most recent data suggests that more than 90 percent of job seekers turn to job boards to either post a resume or search jobs as the first step in their process.

Searching Jobs

When you search jobs on a job board, you are looking for criteria that you input as desirable for your preferences. By selecting categories, locations, compensation, and education level, you are narrowing down thousands of jobs into a manageable number to scan and apply. There are several types of postings that you should be aware of.

Employer Posts

These are jobs that are added to the boards by the employers either directly or through an xml feed (an automatic posting of positions from the company's own site to the job board). Direct posting simply means someone typed in or copied and pasted the data into the job board. Feeds mean that the data was posted somewhere else (typically the company's own Website) and then automatically added to the job board you are viewing. Either way, be sure you check to see how long the posting has been active (if the job board lists that information). That will tell you how fresh the job is.

Recruiter Posts

These are requisitions that recruiters will advertise for on job boards in hopes of finding a candidate for their open order with a client company. Much like employer posts, they can either be direct posts from the recruiter, or xml feeds. You can usually tell if it is a recruiter post because the company's name is not listed.

Job Aggregator Sites

In recent years, several Websites have popped up that collect job postings from across the Web and publish them all in one place. These aggregators are a great way to limit your time spent bouncing from job board to job board. There is no cost for job seekers, as the aggregators are compensated on a pay-per-click basis from the originating sites. I recommend *Indeed.com*, as the site is very easy to navigate and they seem to have the deepest reach of contributing job boards.

Agents or Alerts

Most job boards will allow job seekers to set up automatic e-mail notifications called Agents or Alerts that are sent out when there is a new posting matching your search criteria. These are a great too, but make sure you have the alerts sent to the e-mail account you set up specifically for your job search so your current employer does not see them.

Posting Your Resume

When you upload and submit your resume online to a job board, your search takes on a whole new life. Be ready to field calls from recruiters, company recruiters, and even some scam artists that have erroneous accounts to gather data from these massive databases. I don't want to scare anyone into not posting, but you should be aware of all the activity that you may encounter.

When to Post

Post your resume as soon as you are ready to go from a passive search to an active search. Remember to remove your resume or profile once you have accepted a position or else you will still get calls from other recruiters. I also recommend that you re-post your resume every week or two to make sure your profile stays active. Some job boards now re-post automatically every time you log in so read the fine print in the terms and conditions when creating your account.

What to Post

If the site you are posting to allows you to upload a file, then by all means do so. Your resume will be indexed and show up better in search strings used by recruiters and employers. A Word file is best, as it is the most commonly accepted format. Some sites only allow you to copy and paste into a dialog box. If you have to go this route, then make sure you clean up your pasted material, as some bullets and fonts will not appear like they did in a Word document.

Confidential Resumes

If you are worried about your current employer finding your resume because you know that they use a particular board, just post somewhere else. Recruiters typically pass by confidential resumes because it makes them take an extra step to be able to contact you. If you are really ready to go active in your search, then you should be ready to publish your contact information. Recruiters really dislike the job-board-created links for confidential resumes, so at least have a link to your private email account.

Where to Post

There are so many job boards on the Web that you could spend an eternity just creating accounts and posting resumes. I recommend a dual approach of using at least one of the big boards and a few niche boards.

- Big Boards: *Monster.com*, *CareerBuilder.com*, and *Hotjobs.com* are the most commonly accessed boards for jobseekers. By posting on these boards, you gain wide national exposure. Conversely, you are thrown in with millions of other candidates and limit your potential for being found.

- Niche Boards: No matter what industry you are in, there is most likely a job board or two that is focused on your segment. These are great resources and you will not have to worry about calls from people outside of your industry, but just remember that the traffic on these sites is far below that of the big boards, and your potential to be found is diminished as such. Geographic niche sites are also good places to post if you are only looking for opportunities in your local area.

Resume Distribution Services

These services will take your resume and e-mail blast it to hundreds or thousands of recipients for a fee. Make sure you review the list before accepting and ask about their distribution frequency and success rates.

- Employer Distribution: Your resume is sent out to corporate recruiters or generic HR e-mail drops, which are e-mail accounts that are not monitored daily, but are set up only to accept resume submissions.

- Recruiter Distribution: Your resume is sent out to recruiters that have opted to receive resumes matching certain search criteria, such as keyword combinations, very specific job titles, or former companies listed as employers.

Social Networking

We all know what a powerful tool social networking is in the marketplace and in our lives. Yet employers across the globe are scratching their heads trying to figure out how to tap into this vast resource as a hiring mechanism. Sure, employers know that they should have a Facebook page, a Twitter following, and a LinkedIn profile; but what they have not realized is what to do with it to solve their problem—how to attract, retain, and develop talent for their organization.

Personal Brand

Some of you may be familiar with this buzz term. Your personal brand refers to the process by which people market themselves and their careers. In the past, many self-help books were focused on improving one's performance or outlook on the future. Conversely, the new concept of personal branding suggests that your success will stem from how well you package or present yourself across all media outlets. Personal branding is most often tied to how well an individual can apply his or her name to well-known products. However, personal branding can also extend to your appearance, your published work products, videos of yourself on YouTube, and any other media that documents your track record of success. By building a social media campaign on yourself, you are developing your personal brand.

The two things you should know about social networking and job searches are:

- Most recruiters and employers have some type of program to reach candidates through social networking. If you do not have a social networking presence, you are limiting you chances of being found.

- Employers are increasingly turning to social media to gain insight into the professional and social behavior patterns of applicants. While there is voluminous legislation regarding what can and cannot be done during interviews, and regarding what scope background checks can cover, the door is still wide open on the use of social networking to determine an applicant's fit for a position.

Search the Internet, and you are bound to find several stories about how social networking caused someone to lose their job or not get the job he or she wanted.

Following are three of the most popular social networking tools used by recruiters and employers to find candidates. The list is by no means all-inclusive, but it should give you a start on your personal social networking campaign and personal brand management.

LinkedIn (*www.linkedin.com*)

What It Is

Think of LinkedIn as the business world's answer to social media. There are other sites like it, most notably *Spoke.com*, but this one is the widely accepted leader in the field. It is a free site that allows you to connect to people you know and view their work history and current projects they are working on. It also allows you to see profiles of anyone else on LinkedIn, and gives you ways to connect to them by "linking" through shared people. Think of it as an online version of the Six Degrees of Separation game.

How It Helps

LinkedIn is a haven for company and third-party recruiters looking for the ever-elusive passive candidate—the happily employed and not actively looking for a new position, but could be swayed to a new opportunity. It is also a great place to show potential employers how well you network, as they can see the level of people you typically connect with.

Recommendations

People you are connected to can leave comments on your relationship for all to see. Naturally, you get to approve what gets published, so you can keep the comments positive. This is a great forum to gather referrals from former employers, clients, and other business associates you interact with. The more recommendations you have, the better your profile will show up in search results run by employers or recruiters.

Company Search

If you have a specific company you are interested in, LinkedIn will show you people who are connected to other people you know that work there now, have worked there in the past, or have connections that work there. You can then ask your personal contact to connect you. If you upgrade from the free account to a premium paid account, you have the access to directly e-mail people with whom you do not have a contact in common. Some companies also have company profiles (this is a fairly new feature, so not all businesses will have them) that show demographics about their employees and typical career tracks.

Job Postings

Many recruiters and employers have turned to LinkedIn to post their jobs. These positions are typically mid-level sales or management and above. Job postings are not cheap for employers on LinkedIn, so if you see one on there, you know it is a priority for them.

What You Are Working On

This simple dialog box appears at the top of the page and is seen by every person that looks at your profile. If you are looking for employment, just type in "Searching for a new job opportunity" and recruiters will start salivating.

Links to Your Brand

If you are really on top of your game, you will make use of LinkedIn's capability that lets you link your blog and Twitter account directly to your profile. Updates are done automatically, so you don't have to cut and paste every time you publish content.

Groups

One of the best ways to illustrate your experience in a field is by joining one of the thousands of groups LinkedIn offers to let you connect with others in the same area of expertise. There are groups for school alumni, current and former employers, industry associations, and general business interests.

What to Avoid

As with any social networking site, the most annoying aspect is unqualified, unsolicited requests to connect. The same holds true for LinkedIn, but you are encouraged to reach out to as many people as possible, as long as you share a common thread.

LIONs

I am particularly annoyed by requests from LinkedIn Open Networker (LION) members that want to connect for no apparent reason. There are some LION members that do not obey the unwritten rules, so just be careful before you accept invitations.

Incomplete Profile

Remember that LinkedIn is a widely used tool for recruiters, so you want to make sure that your profile is complete. Use your resume as a starting point and build on it from there.

Twitter (*www.twitter.com*)

What It Is

Twitter is a highly addictive social networking platform that allows users to connect and share short bursts of text (140 characters or less) to share with their followers what they are doing or thinking about.

How It Helps

- Fast Network Development—With Twitter, you can easily create a vast network of people you want to connect with. The more people you follow, the higher the chance that they will follow you.

- Recruiters—Follow as many as possible when you are engaged in your search. You can follow company recruiters or third-party recruiters in your area of expertise. Many of the jobs that they tweet never make it to a job board, so you might pick up on an opportunity the general public will never see. At a minimum, the recruiters will tweet links to the posting on another site, but at least you will see it first.

What Are You Doing?

The whole premise of Twitter is to share your thoughts, actions, or desires with your following. Believe it or not, people want to know what you are doing. Be proactive and share positive comments about your job search like "I had a great interview today" or "I am very impressed with the team at Company XYZ." Letting your followers know about your progress will keep you on their minds, and they might forward your links to similar opportunities.

What to Avoid

- Negative Tweets—Even if your current job is a complete nightmare, refrain from tweeting about it. Nothing good can come from this. If you really need to discuss your current negative situation, do it with someone you trust, and never put it in writing.

- Personal Tweets—Tweeting about where you are eating lunch may be of interest for some, but hold off on personal tweets when you are in the middle of a job search. Everything you put in print is open game for your potential employer to read.

- Too Many Tweets—As addicting as Twitter can be, you should refrain from tweeting every five minutes. If a potential employer sees that you are a Twitter addict, then he or she will think twice before putting you on the clock!

Facebook (*www.facebook.com*)

What it is—originally launched as an online tool for Harvard undergrads to view profiles of their classmates, it has evolved into one of the largest social networking sites in the world.

How It Helps

- Notes—By posting a short comment on your job search, your friends will all see what you are doing. Notes tend to stay on your friend's screens longer than a status update, and you can include more content.

- Status Updates—Similar to Twitter, you should update your status with positive comments about your job search so employers and recruiters can check your interest level. Your friends will also see your status and may pass along other opportunities.

- Tags—If you write a blog post that includes a reference to friends on Facebook, tag them. That way, their friends will be alerted to your post, and your message will spread more quickly.

What to Avoid

- Personal Pictures—Many people use Facebook to post pictures from various events throughout their lives to share with others. When actively interviewing, ask yourself the question, "What would my potential employer think of this picture?" If you have to think twice, then take it down temporarily. In general, pictures of family and friends are acceptable. Conversely, any pictures that show alcohol consumption, political views, or degrading pictures of the opposite sex are off limits.

- Privacy Settings—All the platforms mentioned here have them. The easiest way to avoid a social networking goof is to adjust your Privacy Settings to friends only, or approved members only during your career search.

You are now ready to move on to the actual interview. The next section covers some basic guidelines for behavior and logistics that I call Interview Mechanics.

CHAPTER 2

• • • • •

Interview Mechanics

The subtle nuances that transpire during an interview can have a huge impact on the interviewer's perception of your ability to succeed with their company. Every situation is different and every interviewer has his or her own particular style. The information in this section contains general guidelines for success.

The most important thing you should remember is that the old adage "You never get a second chance at making a first impression" is especially accurate when it comes to interviewing. When you meet your interviewer, make sure you give a firm handshake, look your interviewer in the eye, smile, and clearly state your name. Set the tone by displaying a positive and enthusiastic attitude right from the start.

You should also win over the receptionist or the interviewer's assistant, as these people often have more influence than most people realize. As a former hiring manager,

I have seen several occasions where candidates for employment have blown their chances by treating the other employees in a disrespectful manner.

• • •

A good friend of mine is a hiring manager for a well respected national uniform rental business. Being a believer in his company's products and service, he sometimes wore a work uniform as his daily attire. One day, while dressed in his uniform, he was preparing to interview a candidate that was due to arrive during the lunch hour. The receptionist typically had interview candidates complete an application prior to announcing their arrival and walking them back for their interviews. On that particular day, one of the other office staff was celebrating an anniversary and the office team members all took her out to lunch. As a result, no one was left watching the front desk. Anticipating the arrival of his interview candidate, the hiring manager decided to sit at the receptionist's desk to greet his candidate. When the candidate arrived, the hiring manager greeted him, "Hello, you must be Bill. Please fill out this application and then we will get started with your interview." The candidate, thinking the guy in the work clothes was just a lowly worker replied, "I don't have to fill out an application. I am here for a salaried position." The hiring manager then said, "I understand, but we do require that all employment candidates complete an application for our files." The candidate then dug his own grave by stating, "You obviously don't understand. Just get me your manager or someone that can speak to my level." The hiring manager then handed him his card, introduced himself, and told the candidate that he was right, he did not need to fill out an application because there would be no interview.

•

What to Bring

Over the years, I have seen candidates bring some very unique items with them on interviews—some good, some not so good. The following list should cover most situations, but if you are unsure about whether you need a particular item, just ask your interviewer in advance.

Professional Organizer

A clean, folio-sized portfolio with a notepad is a very professional way to organize your materials. You can find a variety at your local office supply store.

Pen and Pencil

Always bring both to an interview. You should have your pen out to take notes during the interview, and a pencil comes in handy if you have to take any tests.

Resume

As previously mentioned, have your resume ready, but do not present it unless asked and if you are on an interview set up by a recruiter, then make sure you have the same version that the recruiter sent over.

Reference Sheets

Your references should be ready to present, if asked.

Flash Drive

Keep your flash drive with all your scanned supporting documents in your pocket in case your employer asks for a hard copy of a document that you do not have printed out. This way you will save time and demonstrate your efficiency and organization.

Brag Book

As we discussed under documentation, you should have a copy of at least the contents that you can leave with the interviewer.

List of Questions

You should have a list of questions written out and in your portfolio. See page 125 for examples.

Driver's License

Many employers will make a copy of your identification when they submit your information for a background check.

What NOT to Bring

Just as important as what you should bring is the list of items you should not bring. Here are the most common items brought into interviews that should be left in your car.

Phone

This is the absolute worst thing you can bring to an interview. Bringing your phone tells your employer that your time and focus is not dedicated to the interview and that you are easily distracted. Leave it in your car—no exceptions!

Purse

I know, some of you view your purse as a fashion accessory and not a device designed to carry your belongings. Whatever you reasons for carrying a purse may be, set them aside for the interview. For every job seeker I have that argues with me about this, I have just as many hiring managers that tell me how annoyed they are when a candidate brings a purse to an interview. Many view a purse as an item that represents possible external distractions that could be carried over into the workplace.

Keys

Obviously you have to bring these with you to get back into your car but they should stay in your pocket. Do not drop them on the interview's desk. If you have a huge ring of keys and cannot fit them in your pocket, just remove the one key you need and leave the rest in your car.

Research Materials

All the preparation work you did on the company is great, but leave it at home. If you do a good job working in your knowledge of the company and asking solid company questions, the interviewer will know you conducted your research. Memorize what you can and take some handwritten notes on your notepad for anything else you cannot commit to memory.

• • •

I was interviewing for several new account executives for our company and I attended a career fair that allowed companies to conduct a brief the prior evening for all interested candidates. I had a packed room, but could easily determine the top two to three candidates by their demeanor, questions, and impact presence. At the conclusion of my briefing, I adjourned to the hotel bar for a beer. It was towards the end of the afternoon and several of the job seekers I had just briefed had also decided to partake in Happy Hour. Naturally, I engaged in a conversation with several of them and continued the question and answers session we had just left in the briefing room. I had an audience of five to six candidates, one of whom I was really interested in, and I purchased a round of drinks for the group. After a few more questions, I excused myself and retired for the evening to prepare for a full day of interviews the next day. That next day, I checked my schedule and saw that the candidate I was very excited about was due to interview in my hotel room with me later that morning. When he knocked on my door at the appointed time, he looked sharp, but was carrying something that forced me to do a double take to believe my eyes. In his hands were two bottles of beer. He shook my hand and said, "You bought me a beer last night and I am a man that always repays my debts, so I thought I would give you a beer to settle up!" He then sat down, opened his beer, and took a long pull from the bottle. I politely thanked him for the beer and set mine aside to conduct what turned out to be a very short interview. While I appreciated his gesture, it was entirely inappropriate to bring a beer to an interview!

•

Do's & Don'ts

Here are a few more items that are worth mentioning when you are preparing for your interview.

Do's

- Confirm: If your interview involves travel or was set more than two days in advance, call to confirm the day prior.

- Thank your interviewer: It is polite to thank your interviewer for his or her time before you get started.

- Shake hands: Always accept a handshake if offered by your interviewer, and offer one even if not presented to you.

- Maintain posture: Skilled interviewers are also experts on body language, so be sure to sit upright and maintain a good posture.

- Maintain eye contact: Always look your interviewer in the eye when speaking.

- Display enthusiasm: Your attitude sets the tone for the entire interview. Smile often and say things like:

  ➲ "I am excited to be here!"

  ➲ "I am thrilled to interview for this opportunity!"

  ➲ "This is exactly what I have been looking for!"

Don'ts

- Be late: Make sure you understand the local traffic patterns and give yourself plenty of time to arrive at your destination 15 minutes prior to your scheduled appointment. If an unforeseen event does occur, call your interviewer and let them know.

- Get casual: It is common courtesy to stand until either you are asked to be seated or sit after your host seats themselves. Keep your suit coat on unless the interviewer tells you that you may remove your coat. Do not slouch or lean over when seated.

- Complain: Good interviewers pick up on everything you say. Even casual references to heavy traffic, a bad morning, or a hectic schedule are all seen as negatives by the interviewer.

Attire

How you present yourself on an interview is just as important as what you say. An old coach of mine used to say "If you look good, you feel good. If you feel good, you play good. If you play good, you win!" That same adage holds true for interviewing. The image you present carries over to your confidence level and your performance is a direct result. I have assembled these quick lists for a general reference on attire. If you still have questions regarding what to wear, your best solution is to consult a professional at a well known business attire retail store. Be sure to tell the sales associate that you are purchasing interview attire and that you want a conservative combination that conveys self confidence and professionalism.

When going on a professional interview, always assume the dress is business professional, unless told otherwise. If your scheduled interview is a plant tour or day in the field, then be sure to ask the person setting up the interview if the dress is professional or business casual.

If your interview requires you to travel, be sure you steam out the wrinkles in your suit the night before. An old trick is to run a hot shower and hang your suit in the bathroom to let the steam work out the wrinkles. This works in an emergency, but a travel iron is better. If you are flying in for a same-day interview, carry your suit jacket with you and ask the one of flight attendants to hang it up for you. My experience is that even if you are not flying first class, if you ask nicely and tell them you are on your way to an interview, they will almost always hang it up for you.

• • •

One of our recruiters had a candidate scheduled for a final interview that involved traveling to the potential employer's headquarters building. Shortly after the scheduled interview time, our recruiter called the hiring manager at the business to ask how the candidate performed during the interview. The hiring manager said that she had never interviewed a more qualified candidate and was equally impressed with his enthusiasm and developmental potential. She then went on to say that she was extremely disappointed that she could not make him an offer because of his complete lack of professionalism when it came to his attire. To quote, "He looked like a wrinkle bomb exploded directly on him." When our recruiter called the candidate to let him know that he would not be getting the offer, he naturally asked why and admitted that he had not had time to prepare his garments before the interview, but didn't think that it would really make a difference—it did!

•

Here are some basics for the different types of business attire:

Business Professional: Men

- Conservative Suit: Dark, solid color or a dark color with a faint pinstripe.

- Shirt: White or blue long-sleeved dress shirt.

- Tie: Conservative pattern that hangs to the top of your belt.

- Footwear: Dark socks that match your suit, professional leather shoes that match your belt.

- Jewelry: Keep this to the bare minimum. Typically just a watch and a wedding ring, but a class ring is also acceptable.

- Grooming: Neat, professional hairstyle, trimmed nails, fresh shave.

Business Professional: Women

- Conservative Suit: Dark, solid color or a dark color with a faint pinstripe.

- Blouse: Coordinated with suit, but stick to a conservative solid pattern or stripe. Avoid pinks and purples, as some interviewers view it as too feminine.

- Shoes: Avoid open-toed shoes and heels higher than 2 inches.

- Jewelry: Less is better, and avoid earrings that dangle, as they could be distracting.

- Hosiery: Nude or light colored.

- Grooming: Conservative make-up, professional hairstyle, manicured nails, and light perfume.

Business Casual: Men

- Khaki, gabardine, or cotton pants, neatly pressed.

- Cotton, pressed, long-sleeved, button-down shirts, polo or knit shirts with a collar.

- Matching leather shoes and belt (no deck shoes or tennis shoes).

Business Casual: Women

- Khaki, corduroy, twill, or cotton pants or skirts, neatly pressed.

- Sweaters, twinsets, cardigans, polo/knit shirts.

- Solid colors work better than bright patterns.

- Solid-colored pumps with conservative heels.

Interview Attire Tips—Do's

- Fit: Make sure everything fits correctly and has been recently tailored.

- Preparation: Get your clothes ready the night before, so you don't have to spend time getting them ready on the day of the interview. Remember to iron your shirt.

- Clean: If your clothes are dry clean only, take them to the cleaners after an interview, so they are ready for next time.

- Scuffs: Inspect your belt and shoes for any scuff marks and polish accordingly.

- Breath: Bring a breath mint and use it just before you enter the building.

Interview Attire Tips—Don'ts

- Uniform: never wear any part of your military uniform (tie clips, badges, belts).

- Shoes: It is generally known that men should not wear a brown belt or shoes with a blue suit; women should not wear stiletto heels on an interview.

- Shirt: Men should never wear a short-sleeved shirt with a suit, sport coat, or tie; women should never wear a sleeveless blouse if they intend on taking their jackets off.

- Lapel Pins: Refrain from supporting your causes or charities during the interview process.

- Grooming: Go easy on the perfume, aftershave, or cologne.

Body Language

Whether you know it or not, your body language speaks volumes to the interviewer. Once you understand the most common tips and techniques used in subtle body language, you can use them to influence your interviewer. Body language can be a simple pose, your posture, your seated position, or even how you use your hands during conversation. When it comes to interview preparation, you should video yourself doing a short mock interview for 10 to 15 minutes to see what your body language says. After you are done, turn off the volume and watch yourself to see if you can figure out what you are saying based on your movements. You will be amazed what you find. Almost every time I have done this with candidates, they immediately recognize a bad habit, such as crossing their arms, or repeatedly running their hands through their hair. Here are some tips from the bottom up to help you when evaluating your body language.

Feet

Keep both of your feet on the floor. Crossing your legs can send a message of complacency or over confidence.

Legs

It is okay if you are a bit nervous during an interview, but try not to show it through your energy. The most common form of this is when job seekers constantly bounce their legs up and down or cross their legs and shake their feet. Not only is it distracting to the interviewer, but you also send the message that you lack the ability to stay focused—not an admirable trait in a future employee.

Walk Fast

From the moment you exit your car to walk into the building, you should walk at a brisk pace. An old trick by some sales interviewers is that they will greet interviewees at the door and walk them back to their office at a fast pace. If the interviewees fail to keep pace, then they most likely lack the energy required to succeed in sales.

Sit Forward

By leaning slightly forward in your seat, you tell the interviewer that you are interested and that you are actively listening. When you lean back in your seat, your body is telling the interviewer that you are disinterested or that you are cocky, neither of which is good.

Hands in Pockets

When on an interview, the only time your hands should enter your pockets it to put something in or pull something out. Walking with your hands in your pockets shows too casual of an attitude and conveys to the interviewer that you are not interested. When you put your hands in your pockets when seated, it looks sloppy and unprofessional. I do suggest that you keep a business card in your left pocket in case the interviewer asks you for a card. That way you can quickly reach in with your left hand, leaving your right hand free for a handshake if the interview is winding down. If you are wearing a skirt, or do not have a pocket for a business card, be sure you have one easily accessible in your portfolio or note-taking materials.

Folded Arms

Any body language interpreter will tell you that folded arms means you are not interested and may even be holding back some degree of anger or disagreement with the person you are communicating with. Interviewers will see folded arms as a negative, even though you might be verbally agreeing with them.

Folded Hands

The safest bet is to rest your hands, lightly folded on the desk in front of you. Another trick is to hold a pen or pencil to show that you are ready to take notes as needed. Do not click the pen constantly or twirl it around your fingers. If you do not have a desk or table in front of you, then place your hands in your lap, one hand on each leg, or folded lightly. Above all else, keep your hands away from your face.

Rubbing Your Neck

When you stretch in an interview or rub the back of your neck, you are telling the interviewer that you have lost interest. Keep your hands in front of you and on the desk or table.

Touching Your Nose

Many experts will tell you that if you touch your nose during a conversation, that is a tell for dishonesty. It is also disgusting, and the interviewer will not want to shake hands with you after you do this.

Fingers Through Your Hair

When you run your fingers through your hair, you are telling the interviewer that you are stressed and tired.

Looking at Your Watch or the Door

Never look at your watch or the door during an interview, as it says you have somewhere more important to be. If you have legitimate time constraints, then tell the interviewer before you get started. The only acceptable reason is travel schedules, not picking up the kids from school or an appointment with your personal trainer.

Eye Contact

The absolute best way to show the interviewer that you are interested and engaged is to look him or her directly in the eye. When you fail to make direct eye contact, the interviewer never connects with you and you miss out on a key advantage over other candidates.

Most experts agree that initiating and maintaining eye contact for periods of at least eight to 10 seconds suggests active listening skills. It is perfectly acceptable to glance away and reestablish every so often, so as not to appear to stare down the person with whom you are speaking.

Avoid looking down, as you come across as submissive and it shows that you lack confidence. It is okay to look down at your notepad if you are taking notes, but glance up every few seconds to keep the eye contact and to show you are still listening.

10 Common Pitfalls

This list represents the top ten reasons companies provide for choosing not to pursue a candidate after at least one interview:

10. Lack of Personality: If your communications are dry and you fail to show an ability to engage others, employers will find it hard to get excited about you. If you lack self-confidence or are introverted, you will need to make a conscious effort to overcome these areas to show the interviewer your personal style.

9. Lack of Industry Interest: If you are looking at several different industry sectors, then don't tell your interviewer that another industry is your ideal career track. Make sure the interviewer knows that this opportunity and industry are your number one focus, even if it is your fall-back opportunity. Make sure you also know all the major players within the industry and what separates the company from its competitors.

8. Poor Communication Skills: Not providing succinct, direct answers to the interviewer's questions is often

cited, but simple things like lack of eye contact, not speaking clearly, or excessive "ums" and "ahs" will also prevent your progression.

7. Poor Impact Presence: A sloppy attire or an unkempt appearance is typically a show-stopper. Interviewers know that you will never look any better than on your interview, so you should look pretty sharp to make that first impression. Also, remember to mimic the corporate culture in terms of attire as best as possible.

6. Geographic Limitations: this could be a show-stopper, not just for the current opportunity, but for longer-range growth within the company if you are not willing to relocate later for an advancement opportunity.

5. Career Plan: If you are not able to relay your long-range career goals, then the interviewer will see you as short-sighted. Additionally, an unrealistic goal (like making CEO of a Fortune 500 company four years out of college) will get you escorted to the door promptly.

4. Lack of Company Research: Remember that if you fail to prepare, you are also preparing to fail. Your research efforts will pay a big dividend if you just put in the time.

3. Lack of Enthusiasm: This could be a lack of visible interest in the job or in general. Make sure you smile and express to the interviewer that you are excited about the position.

2. What's in it for me? Too much focus on salary and benefits too early in the process is a very common mistake that really annoys hiring managers. The initial interviews are for the employer to learn more about your experiences and skills, not what you require from your potential employer.

1. No Specific Examples: More than all the other reasons combined, the lack of specific examples when answering interview questions is the number one reason candidates are eliminated from the interview process.

If you are surprised at the number one reason why candidates do not move forward in the interview process, then you are not alone. The entire SOAR Method, which you will learn in the next section, is centered on teaching you how to provide specific examples when answering interview questions. In Chapter 3, you will see exactly where this comes into play and how to recognize when you should apply the SOAR Method.

• • • • •

Phases of the Interview

If you are like most job seekers, you have had very little professional training on how to win interviews. Some of you may have undergone some training when you graduated college, moved on from your last career, or left the military, but you still feel that you are missing something. In this section, I take the skills and tactics that companies use and show you how, by applying our unique method, you can deliver exactly the type of responses employers are looking for.

Companies spend millions of dollars every year learning how to attract, identify, develop, and retain talent. If you are interviewing, then they have attracted you. Our focus is on the identification of talent. Once you are hired, they will attempt to develop and retain you.

Whether you realize it or not, you will go through several phases during your interview. While the order and duration of each phase will vary slightly from one interviewer to the next, most initial screening interviews follow this pattern that interviewers are taught during their talent identification training. The better the interviewer, the smoother the transition from phase to phase.

- Rapport Building
- Background Information
- Confirming Requirements
- Behavioral Questions
- Questions for the Interviewer
- Closing Questions and Methods

Rapport Building

You will be asked some tough questions. Know this going in, and you will be ready for anything. Relax and focus on the opportunity in front of you. Most screening interviews are not designed to find qualified candidates, but rather to rule out non-qualified candidates.

The rapport building phase is also known as the Meet and Greet period of the interview. You can expect the interviewer to use a conversational tone and put you at ease. In this phase, the interviewer is attempting to get a conversation started by asking some ice-breaker questions.

Some of the questions you can expect in this phase include:

- How is your day going?
- Did you have a good morning?
- Were the directions okay?

- Were you waiting long?

- How far did you travel to get here?

Keep your answers brief—this is not the time to start reciting your work history or explaining why you are the perfect fit for the position.

Keys to Success

- Smile and display enthusiasm.

- Be confident and give a firm handshake.

- Thank the interviewer for his or her time.

- Ask the employer how his or her day is progressing.

- Keep your responses brief.

This phase typically lasts two to five minutes and transitions directly into the Background Information phase.

Background Information

In this phase, the interviewer will attempt to gain basic biographical information about you. This phase is also a test to see how concisely you can deliver your personal elevator pitch. This is a two to three minute summary of who you are. You will recognize you are in this phase when the interviewer asks a question or requests you to provide your background with a statement like one of the following:

- Tell me about yourself.

- What's your background?

- Give me your two-minute life story.

- Walk me through your resume.

These are open-ended questions or requests for information. When presented with an open ended question, most candidates do not recognize it and either one of two things happen, neither of which is good.

- The candidate starts fumbling because he or she has not prepared or rehearsed, and says something completely off the mark like, "It's all on my resume" or "Didn't you look at my resume yet?"

- The candidate dives into a 20-minute soliloquy detailing every aspect of his or her life without stopping once to come up for air.

When presented with an open-ended question, you should provide a brief verbal presentation on your professional career to date. If you are a recent college graduate, then you would simply substitute your college experiences and academic highlights in lieu of work experience.

Keys to Success

Preparation

Develop an outline to help you piece together your key selling points—short statements that relay why you made the decisions you made and how they impacted your career progression.

Introduction (30 seconds)

- ➲ Start with college or HS.

- ➲ Explain any geographical moves.

- ➲ Remember to use the same reverse chronological approach you used when drafting your resume.

"Thanks for asking! I was born and raised in the Washington D.C. area and excelled at sports and academics in high school. I decided to attend college on the west coast to gain some exposure to another region of the country and was admitted to UCLA on a partial academic scholarship. I was very active at UCLA and participated in several clubs and intramural sports activities. I selected Business Administration as my major and graduated with honors in four years."

Body (1–2 minutes)

- ➲ Briefly touch on major accomplishments in your work history. We are just touching the wave-tops here, not delivering detailed examples yet.
- ➲ Say what you accomplished.
- ➲ Share why you did it (demonstrates your decision making process).
- ➲ Show how effective your actions were.

(Item 1: What You Did) "After college, I joined a small start-up firm in San Diego as a Project Manager for their initial round of fund raising for investment capital to launch a new software product."

(Item 1: Why You Did It) "I choose this opportunity over several other offers because it gave me the exposure to project management, investor relations, and financial reporting that would allow me to see the whole cycle a start-up business goes through.

(Item 1: Key Selling Point) "My efforts in developing the formal business plan and forecasts were instrumental in the company securing its initial funding in excess of $2.4 million for the product launch.

(Item 2: What You Did) "After two years with that organization, I moved on to join a national retail outlet and performed several roles in two different store locations, including Assistant Store Manager, Loss Prevention Manager, and Customer Service Manager.

(Item 2: Why You Did It) "The reason I chose this path was to continue my professional development by getting more corporate experience through a formalized leadership development program with a nationally recognized company.

(Item 2: Key Selling Point) "The experience I gained with this company has given me a solid understanding of how to lead teams and inspire others to perform in less than optimal conditions."

Close (30 seconds)

- ➲ Share how these experiences translate into value to the employer.

- ➲ Explain what put you on the market.

- ➲ State why you are interested in this position.

(How Skills Translate) "I believe that my diverse skills and experiences to date have made me a well rounded manager and an inspirational leader. **(Why You are Looking)** I am looking for a new opportunity that will provide me with a cultural match and challenge me to achieve new levels of performance. **(Interest in Position)** I am very interested in this opportunity, as I can see that it not only presents the environment to achieve but also has a track record of exceeding shareholder expectations year after year."

Rehearse

Be sure you are comfortable with your presentation, but you do not have to memorize it word for word. Slight variations in wording are fine, as long as you remember your key selling points.

- ➲ Time your response: 2–3 minutes total.

- ➲ Record your response and listen to yourself.

➲ Voice inflection: Do you trail off at the end of your sentences or finish just as strong as the start?

➲ Count your "Ums" and "Ahs" and keep rehearsing until you are at zero.

Narrative Presentation Outline Guide

Introduction

School/Home: _____

_____

_____

_____

Body

Item 1

What you did: _____

_____

_____

Why you did it: _____

_____

_____

Key selling point: _____

_____

_____

Item 2

What you did: _____

_____

_____

Why you did it:_____

_____

_____

Key selling point: _____

_____

_____

Item 3

What you did: _____

_____

_____

Why you did it:_____

_____

_____

Key Selling Point: _____

_____

_____

Close

How your skills translate:_____

_____

_____

Why you are looking: _____

_____

_____

State interest in position: _____

_____

_____

Illegal Questions

There are some questions that interviewers would love to ask, but are not allowed. These questions often manifest during the Background Questioning phase. Offer up as much detail as you feel comfortable with, but remember that you are under no requirement to answer.

If you are asked a question you know is illegal, do not say, "That is an illegal question." Rather, simply respond by saying, "I'm really not sure how that relates to the position," then move on to the next topic. Another trick is to turn the question back on the interviewer. For example, if an interviewer asks if you have children, you can respond by saying, "It sounds like a good work home/balance is something you value. How do you manage the demands of home and work?"

Here are some of the more common questions interviewers would love to be able to ask, the tactics they use to get the desired answer without really asking, and some suggested responses:

Do you smoke?

Some interviewers will even ask the candidate if they would like to join them for a cigarette just to see what their response is, and then move on to something else.

What country are you from?

While it is acceptable to ask if you are legally able to work in the United States or if your work requires sponsorship, it is way off limits to ask where you are from, your native language, or when you came to the United States. If you encounter this question, just state that you are legally able to work in the United States.

Are you married?

A less aggressive approach interviewers take is to ask, "What do you like to do in your free time?" They are looking to see what type of activities you do outside the workplace to determine if you are a family-oriented person. Either way, it is an area that they really have no business asking about because it does not directly relate to your abilities to perform the job. Most candidates offer this information up anyway, as they think it is just an icebreaker question.

Are you a Christian/Jew/Muslim?

Most of the time, these questions arise when interviewers are attempting to determine your availability due to religious holidays or observances. Respond by stating, "My personal affiliations will in no way interfere with my work schedule. Are there any days in particular you are concerned about scheduling?" If that does not work and they persist, fall back on, "I'm really not sure how that relates to the position."

Do you have children?

Employers want to know this because they want to see if you are a single parent, or if you have certain restraints on your schedule relating to childcare. I know of several interviewers that will break out pictures of their children in hopes that the candidates will then open the dialog. Once you open the topic, they have free reign to ask about your situation. Use the work/home balance rebuttal to deflect.

How old are you?

This one is more common on phone interviews, but I have seen it in face-to-face interviews as well. It is very unlikely that an interviewer will be this direct, but rather ask about the years you attended college to try and do the backwards math to determine your age. The best response I have ever heard from a candidate was, "I have 20 years of solid work ethic left in me before I can even think about retirement." This response demonstrates commitment, but deflects the actual question without agitating the interviewer.

Do you plan on having children?

This question is typically encountered by young female job seekers, but I have heard of interviewers asking males as well. Strangely enough, it is most often asked by other females. Interviewers are looking to see your commitment level, not your personal family planning goals. Their view is that they are going to spend time training you and getting you up to proficiency. They do not want to then lose you immediately after the expense of training for an extended leave period or possibly even permanently. Your response should follow this example. "That is a topic for my husband (or wife) and I to discuss in private, but I can assure you that my commitment to my career goals and in adding value to this organization are paramount."

Have you ever been arrested?

While it is perfectly acceptable to ask a job seeker if her or she has ever been convicted of a felony or has had any DUI convictions, it is not legal to ask if you have been arrested. Remember, we are innocent until proven guilty (convicted) in this country! If asked in this manner, simply reply by stating that you have never been convicted of any felonies or DUIs.

Are you still in the military reserves?

This is a legal question, but a very gray area for employers, as many will go beyond the simple question and ask about military drill dates and upcoming reserve commitments. It is illegal for an employer to discriminate against a member of any branch military reserves or National Guard.

Ninety-nine times out of 100, interviewers ask these questions, not as a direct attempt to discriminate, but to develop a dialog. Most interviewers are not even aware of the legality concerning these questions. However, if you think that the questioning was a deliberate attempt to discriminate against you from attaining the position, then you should be aware of your rights. You have the option to file a charge of discrimination with the Equal Employment Opportunity Commission (EEOC). A further review of the EEOC Website will let you know whether or not you should proceed.

This phase usually takes about five to seven minutes and flows directly into confirming requirements.

Confirming Requirements

In this phase, the interviewer wants to make sure that you are after the same type of position and work environment as the opportunity you are interviewing for. These are what I call show-stopper questions because if your responses here do not align with the interviewer's needs, there really is no reason to further the interview process.

Skilled interviewers will confirm their requirements early so as not to waste their time with a two-hour interview, only to find out that you do not meet their basic needs. Here are three show-stoppers that will preclude you from moving further in the process:

Geography/Relocation

While we all have our wish list, you must know what location(s) the interviewer is sourcing for before you start the interview. If you say "I can only live in Dallas," and the position or positions are not in Dallas, then your interview may be over. Most interviewers will simply ask, "Are you aware that this position is in Los Angeles?"

Overly Eager

If you are relocating or attempting to relocate, do not get so excited about the location of the position that the interviewer might get the impression you want this opportunity solely due to geography. It's okay to state that the area you are discussing is your primary location choice, but follow up with an additional response to confirm that it is not the only reason.

Example:

"Yes, Los Angeles is a perfect location. My spouse grew up here and we love the area. However, I am most excited about this opportunity because of the development potential, not just the geography."

Open to Anywhere

You might be interviewing for a position that has multiple openings across the country. Have your top three to five locations ready to deliver, but also stress that it is the company that excites you most, and that you would be willing to take any location to prove how you will deliver results.

Relocation for Advancement

If the interviewer asks if you are open to relocation, keep the door open for a later discussion. Do not get into specifics yet about when and where. Win the rest of the interview first and let the interviewer want you before you start your negotiations about when to relocate. A great response to this question is, "Of course, I am open to future relocation for advancement based on my performance."

Type of Work

These show-stopper questions will close more doors faster than you can imagine. If you are interviewing for a call center manager position and the interviewer asks "What type of work do you want to do?" Don't say "sales!" Keep your answers targeted directly at the opportunity in front of you.

Purple Sock

Very skilled interviewers will trick you into coughing up your true work type goals by asking about other companies you are interviewing with. I call this the purple sock tactic. Remember when you were a kid and you used to watch Sesame Street and they would show three socks on the screen, and two were green and one was purple? One of these things is not like the other! Employers will easily pick up on the fact that they are the purple sock and no one wants to be the purple sock. For example, you are interviewing for a sales position and the interviewer asks what other opportunities you are currently interviewing for. You reply by listing three project management jobs. The interviewing company is now the purple sock and the interview is over.

Schedules/Shift Work

Another common show-stopper relates to scheduling. Be sure you understand the hours or shifts involved and relay to the interviewer your plan to make this schedule work if it is a non-traditional schedule.

Salary Requirements

In an ideal situation, you will know the compensation range before ever going on the interview. If you are working with a recruiter, he or she should brief you and if you have responded to a posting, the details should be provided in the position description. However, this is not always the case. Often, you only have an idea as to the compensation range and go into the interview with limited information. In either case, this is not the time for salary negotiations; it is a screening question to make sure you are in the same ball park as what the employer is capable of paying for the particular position.

The first time an interviewer asks you about compensation, it is okay to deflect and attempt to move on. Remember that we want to negotiate compensation at the end of the process after the employer really wants you on the team, as you are then negotiating from a position of power. So when asked, just state, "I obviously want to earn a good income but the growth opportunity and cultural compatibility are more important than my initial salary."

If the interviewer asks again, then you need to provide real numbers. Always use a range so you don't sell yourself short or price yourself out of the position. It also tells the interviewer that you are flexible.

Published Rate

If you know the rate for a job board posting or listing on the company's website, then simply state that you are comfortable with the advertised compensation as referenced in the published job description.

Recruiter Briefing

If your recruiter sent you in, make sure he or she gives you a rate or range. I know that some recruiters like to overstate the compensation to get you excited about the opportunity and then they back you into the offer at a lower rate just to close the deal. To avoid this, just tell your interviewer that their recruiter briefed the position at low-end to high-end and that you are comfortable with that range. If the position is outside of that range, he or she will tell you right away and you will know where you stand early on in the process.

Limited Information

When you don't have all the information, it is best to stick close to your most recent earnings and best research regarding the position.

Ranges

Provide real numbers based on what you think the position is paying and on your most recent earnings.

Upshifter

We all want to increase earnings as our career progresses. Some employers will ask what you have earned during the past two years. They want W-2 reported income to see if you are making a gradual step up.

This phase lasts five to 10 minutes and gradually eases you into the meat and potatoes of the interview—the Behavioral Questions.

Behavioral Questions

Remember in the previous section when we counted down the top 10 reasons interviewers choose *not* to pursue a candidate? Remember the number-one reason? Failure to provide specific examples.

Interviewers are taught that the best indicator of your future performance is your pattern of past behaviors. Employers hire on behavior patterns and then teach the specific skills required for the job. If you fail to provide specific examples to demonstrate your behavior patterns, the interviewer will never fully grasp why you make decisions or realize how you attained the results you listed on your resume. The interviewer wants to understand your decision-making process.

The type of questions interviewers ask to determine your behavioral patterns and decision-making process are called behavioral questions. In this section, you will learn how to answer behavioral questions using the SOAR method (see page 113). This phase of the interview is typically the longest phase and can run anywhere from 10 minutes to more than an hour.

"Why should I hire you?"

Even though most interviewers will never be this direct (although some will) they all want to know this and you should be able to respond to this underlying question on every one of your responses. When you provide an answer to an interview question, the specific example you give using the SOAR method shows the interviewer whether or not your behavior pattern will add value to the organization.

Identifying Behavioral Questions

Before we can answer behavioral questions we have to be able to identify them.

Easily Recognized

Some interviewers will let you know they want a specific example by phrasing the questions in a way that leads into offering a SOAR response.

- "Tell me about a time when you…"

- "Give me an example where you…"

Harder to Recognize

Most interviewers want examples in the responses, but don't have the skill to extract them from the candidates. In these circumstances, you have to know when to provide your specific examples using the SOAR method.

- "Why sales?"

- "Describe your leadership style."

- "What is your biggest weakness?"

Most candidates do not recognize these as behavioral questions. By understanding you are in this phase of the interview, you can properly assume that most questions are behavioral in nature. Starting on page 118, we provide a list of typical behavioral questions by job type to help you determine when to provide your SOAR responses.

Theoretical Answers

Most candidates unknowingly respond to behavioral questions with theoretical answers. Theoretical answers explain what you would do or what you think you would do in a certain situation. What they lack are examples of when you have applied the theory to practice. Theoretical answers do not answer the underlying question, "Why should I hire you?" Here are four very common behavioral interview questions and the typical theoretical responses that candidates reply with:

Why Sales?

"Well, I have always known that I would end up in sales because I love people and I love influencing people. All of my friends and colleagues have always told me that I should be in sales because people listen to me. I love the idea of controlling my own income potential and have the work ethic it takes to succeed in a fast paced, competitive environment. I have an incredibly competitive nature, and love to see my name at the top of the list."

Describe Your Leadership Style.

"My leadership style is based on open communication and trust. I firmly believe that as a leader, I should do my best to keep my people informed and include them in the decision-making process whenever possible. Sometimes, however, I know I must be able to make quick decisions for the benefit of the entire team. By communicating with my team on a regular basis, I earn their trust and encourage their contributions to the overall goals of the organization. I believe in praising in public whenever someone does something that helps the group. I also think that when it is time to reprimand or correct someone's actions that it should be done in private. After documenting the conversation, I follow up with specific tasks listed as corrective actions."

What Is Your Biggest Weakness/Area Needing Improvement?

"I really believe that I can improve my patience level. I am always ahead of schedule on deadlines and get irritated when other members of the team do not deliver the same quality results in a timely manner. I guess that is something I could improve, but I am so focused on accomplishing the project or task that I sometimes forget that others may not have the same level of dedication I do."

How do You Handle Stress?

"I think that we all have stress in our lives, but it is how you deal with it that makes you productive. I also believe that every position or job will have situations that create stress for some people. The question you have to ask yourself is, are these the type of stressors that I can handle or not? I think that I do a good job of keeping my stress level in check by maintaining a good work/life balance, openly communicating with others involved should a situation start to spin out of control, and by using my resources."

Great answers, right? Wrong! These are perfect examples of theory, not practice. By applying the SOAR Method, you can take the same data and show how, through your actions, you demonstrate the past performance that would lead to your predictive future behavior. We will look at these same four questions and responses again after we learn how to apply the SOAR Method to answer behavioral questions.

Answering Behavioral Questions

Over the years of placing thousands of candidates, I have developed a proven method to convey your specific examples. I know it is hard to remember to give examples on every question, so just use this method and you will succeed, but it takes practice!

The method is centered on you providing real world examples of your past behavior. Remember, past performance is the best indicator of future behavior. Behavioral patterns are what good interviewers are attempting to determine. So, the more specific, relative examples you can give, the better off you are. At the end of the book are some worksheets for you to use in scripting out your SOAR responses. I highly recommend that you do this for the most common interview questions you expect to encounter for your industry and position level. If you do this and rehearse, then when you are presented with the question, you know exactly which SOAR story you can apply to convey your example.

Once you rehearse your SOAR stories to the point where you know them inside and out, you will then have developed the storytelling pattern to create new ones on the fly for those unexpected questions that also need a SOAR response. So, get ready to learn the breakthrough method that will set you apart from the rest of the crowd.

The SOAR Method

Situation

This section sets the tone for the story you are about to relay. Great storytellers all have great lead-in statements. Remember the old fairytales you used to have read to you as a child that all started out "Once upon a time..."? These were examples of setting the situation. It is not only okay to use names and company names here; it is encouraged, as it adds validity to your SOAR stories.

Examples:

- "I had a recent situation at my current employer where I was leading a project team of 12 programmers."

- "I have a great example to share with you about my last team's quarterly sales contest."

- "Just last month I had a discussion with my General Manager, Steve Wilson, regarding improving our group's customer satisfaction index."

Keep this section very brief—one or two sentences maximum. Identify the setting by stating where you were, who was involved, and establish the timeline (when the example occurred), and then move on to the Objective.

The SOAR Method

S	Situation	Briefly describes the background information necessary to relay your specific example. • "For example…" • "Just last month…" • "I had a recent situation where…"	15–20 Seconds
O	Objective	Tells the corrective action to change the behavior, practice, or process. • "My challenge was to…" • "I had a huge task in that…" • "My goal was to…"	15–30 Seconds
A	Action	Relays the steps that were implemented. • "I initiated…" • "I decided to…" • "I developed…"	1–2 Minutes
R	Result	Clearly demonstrates the positive outcome. • "As a result, …" • "At the end of the day/project…" • "At the conclusion of…"	10–20 Seconds

Objective

The dictionary defines objective as the projected state of affairs that a person or a system plans or intends to achieve. In this section, you clearly and concisely state what your desired achievement was at the onset of your example.

Examples:

- "My desired outcome was to reduce our store's shrink rate to 1 percent, which would make my store the lowest in the region, well below our company guideline of 2.5 percent."

- "After attending the sales training event, I committed to myself that I would reach the number-one ranking in the company by the end of the second quarter."

- "I knew that my number-one objective was to reduce our cost of goods sold by 15 percent while maintaining the current revenues to bring my team in line with the company's overall growth strategy."

By stating your objective, you show the interviewer that you understood your goal and set out to achieve it through the planning and actions you will demonstrate in the Action section.

Action

Here you show the steps you took to achieve your Objective. Remember the set of action words we provided on page 29? Flip back and use those same action words to start off your action statements. This is the longest section to the method, but don't go overboard. Cover the main points of what you did and state why you choose that course of action over the other options that were presented or suggested. About three to four sentences should be enough to cover the highlights. If the interviewer wants more detail, he or she will ask. If he or she does ask for more information, then you know that you have his or her interest—great job!

Examples:

- "I set out by first calling a meeting with all my team members to make sure they all understood the time-sensitive nature of the project. Our client needed the deliverable media in less than two weeks and we typically worked a project of this size for four to six weeks. In that meeting, I stressed to the team how important this key client relationship was to our business and that we would all have to step outside our normal comfort zones to meet the deadline. We held status meetings first thing every morning and afternoon and used the conference room as our operations hub, posting timelines and concepts all over the walls. In each meeting, I asked who needed assistance and either stayed late myself to assist or paired them up with other team members. Because the team saw my commitment level, I never once had to ask them to stay late. The day before the deadline, we did a dry run rehearsal in the morning and then fine-tuned for another dry run that evening."

- "I decided to change my standard sales approach with this prospect, because my normal phone call approach was not getting me in front of the decision maker, Mary Jane, the VP of Talent Management. So instead of calling for an appointment, I physically showed up at the company's facility every day, hoping to reach the decision maker. I was still unable to reach her, but on my fourth day of trying, her assistant told me that if I really wanted to get access to her that I should subscribe to her blog post and contribute some relevant content that she might publish, as she would then be more apt to take my call. So that night, I added a link to an article I researched that supported her post and she published it. The next day, I called just to say thank you. Upon hearing that I was a contributor to her blog, I was put right through. That eventually led to a face-to-face appointment."

Using real names and experiences shows your decision-making process. Be sure to list any obstacles you had to overcome and how and why you did not foresee them in your original plan. Once you have outlined the steps you took to accomplish your objective, you are ready to share your results.

Result

Nobody wants to hear a story without a positive outcome, so be ready to take credit for your actions. I know that many of you have a hard time talking about yourself, but this is the one time it is socially acceptable to brag a little. Make sure that the result is in line with your initial objective and keep the communication to one or two sentences.

Examples:

- "After two weeks of this new approach, I saw my closing ratio increase more than 50 percent!"

- "At the end of the quarter, we reached our goal of 20-percent sales growth over the previous quarter."

- "The entire corporation recently adopted the new procedure I implemented, and last month alone the savings were over $128,000."

Results should be about what you did, not what your team or group accomplished. You can mention the team, but your SOAR story should be focused on how you reached your objective.

Application of SOAR Method

Remember the theoretical answers from a few pages ago? Let's circle back and answer them using the SOAR Method.

Why Sales?

Theoretical Answer: "Well, I have always known that I would end up in sales because I love people and I love influencing people. All of my friends and colleagues have always told me that I should be in sales because people listen to me. I love the idea of controlling my own income potential and have the work ethic it takes to succeed in a fast paced, competitive environment. I have an incredibly competitive nature and love to see my name at the top of the list."

SOAR Method Response:

S: "Sales is my passion because I love to influence people. Earlier this year, I sold my concept for a new fund-raising event to my fraternity, which had been doing the same car wash event for years with minimal participation.

O: "My goal was to get 100-percent participation from all active members and raise more money for our charity, the Disabled American Veterans, than ever before.

A: "I set out by describing my vision of selling discount cards for local retailers to other students. I had heard of similar programs at other campuses and thought that the concept would take off here, because there was currently nothing like it. I then asked key members to chair sub-committees to divide the workload. We had a retail group responsible for getting the retailers to agree to a discount, a support group who researched and selected the card printer and designer, and a sales group that consisted of all brothers to sell the cards around campus once they were complete. I was even able to convince several merchants to kick in some free meal coupons to award to the brothers that sold the most cards. I tracked all the card sales and posted the results on our main bulletin board each Sunday evening just prior to our weekly meeting.

R: "We had every brother participate, and at the end of the semester, we had sold more than $13,000 worth of cards. Our previous best from our old car wash was just over $1,000. We even had a waiting list of merchants that wanted to be included on the card for the next semester. The local DAV was so thrilled with our donation that they named our chapter as their benefactor of the year and even sent a letter to our national chapter thanking me personally and recognizing our group efforts."

Describe Your Leadership Style.

Theoretical Answer: "My leadership style is based on open communication and trust. I firmly believe that as a leader I should do my best to keep my people informed and include them in the decision-making process whenever possible. Sometimes, however, I know I must be able to make quick decisions for the benefit of the entire team. By communicating with my team on a regular basis, I earn their trust and encourage their contributions to the overall goals of the organization. I believe in praising in public whenever someone does something that helps the group. I also think that when it is time to reprimand or correct someone's actions that it should be done in private and documents with specific corrective actions cited moving forward."

SOAR Method Response:

S: "My leadership style can best be summarized by a situation I had a few months ago when one of my team leaders came to me with a problem concerning a temporary worker assigned to his group. The temp worker said that she felt she was getting all the bad or unwanted positions in the production flow because she was female and a temp.

O: "My objective was twofold: first and foremost, investigate the claim before it escalated into a formal discrimination complaint and; two, to make sure the temp worker was able to voice her concerns through proper channels.

A: "After letting my team leader, Bob, give me the details of his conversation with Amy, the temp worker, I asked Bob if he was open to having a discussion with all three of us to get to the root cause for her complaint. Bob agreed and I then went out on to the production floor to find Amy. I told her to take a break and come with me into my office for a brief discussion. I started off by reassuring her that she was not in trouble and that we thanked her for voicing her concern to Bob. I then let Bob explain to her that all new temp workers spend the first two weeks working the least desirable positions to learn the entire production flow prior to getting a more permanent work assignment. Amy was relieved to hear it and said that if she had been told that during orientation that she never would have even voiced her concern. I asked Bob to summarize the conversation in writing and asked Amy if she would be fine with signing the summary for our records. She was more than willing to comply.

R: "As a result of the meeting, I followed up with our HR assistant to make sure she had a document in the production orientation packet that explained the initial rotation of positions. Most importantly, I am happy to report that Amy has moved from temp status to a full-time employee and was even named employee of the month last month."

What Is Your Biggest Weakness/Area Needing Improvement?

Theoretical Answer: "I really believe that I can improve my patience level. I am always ahead of schedule on deadlines and get irritated when other members of the team do not deliver the same quality results in a timely manner. I guess that is something I could improve, but I am so focused on accomplishing the project or task that I sometimes forget that others may not have the same level of dedication I do."

SOAR Method Response:

S: "I really believe that I could continue to improve my patience level. The best example I can think of to demonstrate this is a recent group project I was involved in with three other team members where we were tasked with producing design concepts for a billboard advertisement marketing campaign to a client in half the time we typically use to produce the materials.

O: "My challenge was to get each member of our team to contribute their concepts and materials within two business days. Each of these individuals manages several other accounts, and they were not used to producing materials this quickly. When I announced the time requirement, there were several concerns and complaints offered up by the team. I needed to set these concerns aside and focus everyone on the task at hand.

A: "Personally, I am always ahead of schedule on deadlines and am so focused on accomplishing the project or task, that I sometimes forget that others may not have the same sense of urgency as I do. I sent each designer off with the reminder that I would follow-up with them at noon on the suspense date, four hours prior to the delivery deadline to the client. When the time came, two of the three had completed designs ready for client presentation. The third, however, had barely begun her concept sketches. In the past, I would have been angry and demanded that she immediately produce something for presentation. In this instance, I just reminded her of the time-critical nature of this potentially lucrative deal for the company, and asked if she would be able to meet the deadline. She said that she would have her concept to me, but that it would be about an hour late. I told her that would work and that I would try and buy an extra hour of time from the client. I then called the client to reschedule our pitch, telling them that we had one last design they really needed to see.

R: "At the end of the project, we delivered three concept designs to the client. The one they selected was from the team member that was an hour late. We won the account and were successful in getting additional business from the client. I learned a valuable lesson that sometimes a little patience can pay off exponentially."

How do You Handle Stress?

Theoretical Answer: "I think that we all have stress in our lives, but it is how you deal with it that makes you productive. I also believe that every position or job will have situations that create stress for some people. The question you have to ask yourself is, are these the type of stressors that I can handle or not? I think that I do a good job of keeping my stress level in check by maintaining a good work /life balance, openly communicating with others involved should a situation start to spin out of control, and by using my resources."

SOAR Method Response:

S: "I think that we all have stress in our lives, but it is how you deal with it that makes you productive. Last quarter, I was challenged by my supervisor to increase our production numbers by more than 15 percent without any additional labor support or authorized overtime. For most people this would be a very stressful situation!

O: "My goal was to get our entire team to buy into the fact that we could achieve these numbers because I knew that once we believed we could get it done, we would.

A: "Initially, I was a bit concerned about such a huge increase without any additional labor, but decided not to let the challenge affect my work/life balance. Rather than get stressed out about the numbers, I decided to use the nervous energy to show the rest of the team how committed I was by pitching in whenever I could. I knew that all eyes were on me and that if I showed signs of stress, the rest of the team would react negatively. So, I met with the production team at the beginning and end of each shift and posted numerous charts throughout the plant that we updated daily to graph out our incremental progress. I also used my available resources by calling other plant managers from across the company to benchmark on their production flow to get additional ideas on how to increase our efficiency. The information I was able to learn from just a few phone calls really paid off.

R: "By the end of the quarter, we had increased our production numbers by more than 17.5 percent and celebrated with a departmental party."

Keys to Success

Do you see how by simply telling a story and using the SOAR Method as our outline, you can easily demonstrate your behavior pattern?

Worksheets

The best prepared candidates have a matrix of questions and related SOAR stories they want to use that they refer to prior to ever going on an interview. By using the worksheets provided on page 201, you will be leaps and bounds ahead of your competition.

Rehearse

I know talking about yourself in a formatted structure will take some getting used to, but that is why you have to practice and continually refine your interviewing skills. If you have the time and resources, I highly recommend you get a partner to ask you some of the questions on your worksheets, and either use a video or audio recorder to tape your responses. Then review the media to critique yourself.

Each answer should be one to three minutes. Anything less, and you have not covered enough detail. Anything more, and you have lost their interest and shown that you cannot keep your comments concise.

This phase can last anywhere from 10 to 90 minutes, and typically ends when the interviewer asks if you have any questions for him or her.

Questions for the Interviewer

You know you are entering this phase when the interviewer asks, "What questions do you have for me?" or something similar. This tells you that the interviewer is finished with his or her interrogative period and is now ready to entertain your questions about the company or the position. Far too many candidates consider this the final part of the interview. It is not. Good interviewers continue to evaluate you by the questions you ask.

Prior to any interview, be sure you have five to 10 questions written out specific to the company and opportunity. Do your research ahead of time and have your questions ready. It is okay to have questions written down; it even demonstrates your focus. It is also okay to refer to your notes when asking questions. If you do not have any questions or you use the standard, "You answered all of my questions already" you will lose the interview. Do not ruin a great interview by making this simple mistake.

Types of Questions to Ask

Here are some topics that make for good questions:

Company/Culture

By asking about the culture of the organization, you are showing that you care about more than a paycheck and that you want to find a home where you fit in.

Position

Specific questions about the advertised position are encouraged. Most job postings or written descriptions found online are meant to weed out unqualified candidates, not attract the right ones. Ask about daily tasks, responsibilities, and challenges.

Performance/Growth

Another way to show your long-range goals is to inquire on the typical progression for those who meet or exceed expectations. It shows that you expect to be rewarded for your contributions but only when you earn it.

Process

If you are unsure as to the rest of the interview process, just ask, "What is the remainder of the interview process?" Many candidates consider this a closing question but it is NOT—it is a process question.

Types of Questions NOT to Ask

"What's in It for Me?"

This is the most common mistake when it comes to questions for the interviewer. The interviewer is not the least bit concerned with what you want. He or she only wants to see if you meet the company's needs.

Asking questions about compensation, benefits, time off, or perks like gym memberships or tuition reimbursement do not answer the question, "Why should I hire you?" You can always ask for a standard benefit sheet at the appropriate time (when an offer is delivered) that will cover all your personal concerns.

To ensure you do not ask these types of questions, write down all the questions you think are appropriate for the interview. Set the list aside and then look at it again the next day and ask yourself if it (A) has to do with you, or (B) has to do with you adding value to the company. If any of your questions come back with an A response, remove them from your list.

Training

You are being brought on to make an immediate impact. If you focus too much on what your training will involve, the interviewer will get the impression that you will need to have your hand held and become a burden. A single question like, "Does this position have a formalized training program?" is more than enough. Anything more will scare them off.

Already Covered

If you wrote down a question and the interviewer already provided ample response during your conversation, skip it and move on to the next one. This is why I recommend you write down at least five questions.

Public Knowledge

Readily available research material is not meant for questioning. General questions about stock price, competitors, or their industry are too vague and show your lack of preparation.

Phrasing Questions

Use the assumptive position when phrasing questions. By assuming that you are already on the team, you are demonstrating to the interviewer that you do not waste time and that you are already focused on increasing sales, improving profits, or driving customer satisfaction, whatever the case may be.

Example:

- Question without assumptive: What is your location's profit goal for this year?

- Same question with assumptive: What is our profit goal for the location this year?

Here is another example that is a little less assuming, but still removes the invisible barrier between the interviewer and candidate:

- Question without assumptive: How have the current interest rates affected your business?

- Questions with assumptive: How have the current interest rates affected business?

Sample Questions to the Interviewer

Company/Culture

- What are the company's three biggest strategic initiatives for this fiscal year?

- How will we increase market share while maintaining a high level of customer service?

- What opportunities do you see in our marketplace during the next few years?

- What challenges do you see in our industry in the next few years?

- What are some of the new areas of technology being explored? How do you think they will affect the business in the future?

- Can you describe the corporate culture for me?

Position

- To whom would I report and where does this fit into the organizational structure?

- What are the three most common traits of successful people currently in this position?

- How many people will I be leading?

- Tell me about the most successful person you know in the company who is in this type of position and why you think he or she is successful in the role.

- Who are the internal and external customers I would be serving? How would I interact with these customers, and how could I exceed their expectations?

- What are some barriers I could face in this position, and how could I best address them?

Performance/Growth

- How will my performance be evaluated?

- What are some of the traits that would make someone a good candidate for this position?

- What is the career progression track I can expect, assuming peak performance?

- How would I be rewarded as your number-one sales representative?

Process

- What are the remaining steps in the interview process?

- What are the three most important things you are looking for as you evaluate candidates for this position?

- What would a candidate need to do to exceed your expectations?

Your last question should always be a closing question. The next section covers different types of closing questions and why they are important.

Closing Questions and Methods

No matter how you think the interview went, you must always ask for the job! This is true for interviews for all types of positions. Interviewers will naturally think that your interest level is low unless you demonstrate otherwise by telling them you want the opportunity. *Every* interview must be closed at every stage of the interview process, regardless of industry, position title, or interviewer's position.

Closing for Non-Closers

Not all of us are natural-born closers, so we need some help. During my freshman year in college, I was a little intimidated by some of the prerequisites. Chemistry and biology—or any science for that matter—were not my strengths. I was thrilled to read in the course catalogue that there were actually classes for "non-scientists." I remember thinking, "Wow, I can actually do this. Chemistry for non-scientists will get me covered." The same goes with closing. You have to do it no matter how uncomfortable it makes you. If you don't, you will never graduate, progress to the next interview, or win the job.

Different Methods of Closing the Interviewer

Here are several methods I have developed over the years to help candidates overcome their fear of closing. I suggest you try them all out loud and see which one feels most comfortable for you personally. Regardless of which method you use to close the interview, make sure you remember to smile and show enthusiasm towards the position and opportunity.

Isolation

In this method, you attempt to get any potential objections the interviewer might have out in the open to address them right away. Assuming there will be none, you then move in for the close. If the interviewer does have objections, he or she will share them with you and give you the opportunity to address them on the spot. The hardest objection to overcome is the one you don't know about. This method takes that out of the equation.

Examples:

- "Is there anything we covered today that would prevent me from moving forward in the interview process?"

- "I would love to meet the rest of the team, are they available today, or when would you like to schedule our next meeting?"

Set Up

Here you try to align your skills and behavior traits with the ones the interviewer deems most important. Once that is done, you push for the close.

Examples:

- "What are the three most common character traits of your top performers?"

- "Do you think that I have demonstrated my ability in those aspects today?"

- "Awesome, when can I expect the next interview to take place and with whom will I be meeting?"

The more advanced technique associated with this method is when you ask the question earlier in the interview, and then circle back to it as your close.

- "Jim, you previously mentioned that tenacity, teamwork, and initiative are the most common denominators of your top performers. Have I sufficiently demonstrated my tenacity, teamwork, and initiative today?"

- "Awesome, when can I expect the next interview to take place and with whom will I be meeting?"

Assumptive

This takes assurance that the interview went extremely well. This closing technique is typically used in sales interviews, as it demonstrates your confidence and shows your mastery of using the assumptive close.

Example:

- "Thank you so much for your time today, Bill. I think we had a great meeting, and I am already looking forward to making an impact on your team. What would you anticipate as a start date?"

Subtle

Most people end an interview with "What is the next step?" This is not a close, but a procedural inquiry. Spice it up just a bit, and it becomes a close.

Example:

- "What is the next step in the interview process I can expect and when would you anticipate that occurring?"

OR

- "I understand the next step is typically a plant tour. Will I be afforded that opportunity?"

Direct

Much like the assumptive method, this one takes confidence. The direct method puts the interviewer on the spot by asking if he or she perceives a fit.

Example:

- "I am extremely excited about this opportunity. Do you think that I am someone that would be a good fit for your team?"

OR

- "Do you think that I am a match for the opportunity?"

Overcoming Objections

Contrary to popular belief, there is no "Golden Candidate" for a position. Interviewers will have objections about every candidate they meet, including the one that eventually gets the offer. The whole point of the closing phase is to ferret out any potential objection(s) or roadblocks to your potential employment.

What most candidates fail to realize is that when interviewers tell you that they have an "apprehension," a "concern," or even a "challenge" with something in your background it means that they like you and want to give you the opportunity to better explain or position yourself. These are easy objections to deal with because you have been presented with them upfront. The objections that are hard to address are the hidden objections, the ones you are not even aware of that might be holding you back.

Our isolation closing technique does a nice job of getting the objections out into the open so you can address them. From here, you will now need to follow a distinct method to properly overcome the objection and move on with the rest of the process. Anyone that has ever had any sales training might recognize a variation to the ECIR Method of overcoming objections.

The ECIR Method to Overcoming Objections

E	**Emphasize**	Shows the interviewer that you care, that you understand, and that you realize it is a concern for them. • "I can appreciate the fact that..." • "I can understand why..." • "I can respect that..."
C	**Clarify**	Allows you to make the interviewer articulate the objection and communicates an assertion of understanding. Shows you were listening and asks for specifics or details. • "What specifically is it about _____ that concerns you?" • "What specific difficulties do you see with..."
I	**Isolate**	Used to establish that there are no further hidden objectives. Allows you to limit the interviewer to only one objection. • "Is _____ the only thing preventing us from moving forward?" • "What other concerns do you have besides _____ ?" • " _____ aside, what else is holding us up from an offer?"
R	**Reply**	Gain agreement that the objection is no longer a concern once you have addressed the issue head on. • "Okay, so we agree that _____ is no longer an issue, right?" • "Does that properly address _____ to your satisfaction?" • "if I can _____ , then would you _____?"

Example:

Interviewer: "I am a little concerned with your lack of direct business-to-business sales experience."

Standard Response: "I know I don't have much experience, but I am eager to learn and can promise you that I will work harder than any rep you have ever seen to beat your expectations."

ECIR Method Response: The following response says pretty much the same thing, but in a format that is non-combative, shows concern for the interviewers challenge, demonstrates understanding, and casts aside the potential for any future objections.

Emphasize	"I can understand why you might be a bit apprehensive given my lack of direct business-to-business sales experience."
Clarify	"What specific challenges have you seen in the past with less experienced representatives joining your team?"
Isolate	"Just to be clear, is my lack of direct B2B sales experience the only thing preventing us from moving toward an offer?"
Reply	"If I can assure you that I am eager to learn and can promise you that I will work harder than any rep you have ever seen to beat your expectations, would that properly address my lack of experience?"

Example:

Interviewer: "The largest project you have managed to date was only a $100,000 budget. This position is for someone with $1 million-plus experience."

Standard Response: "My experience in the fundamentals of project management, to include a full understanding of scope, feasibility, risk assessment, goal definition, team selection and assignments, delegation of tasks, process control, reporting, and completion through deliverables, will ensure success, regardless of the budget size."

Emphasize	"I can appreciate that you are a bit concerned over the budget size of my last project."
Clarify	"What specific difficulties do you think I would encounter with a larger budget?"
Isolate	"If we took the budget size and set it aside, are there any other challenges you perceive with my experience that you think would prevent me from running this project?"
Reply	"Okay, so aside from the budget of my last project, would you agree that my experience in the fundamentals of project management to include a full understanding of scope, feasibility, risk assessment, goal definition, team selection and assignments, delegation of tasks, process control, reporting, and completion through deliverables will ensure success, regardless of the budget size?"

The End of the Interview

While the closing question usually ends the interview, don't forget to thank the interviewer for his or her time and ask for a business card if you do not already have one. Offer a handshake and exit the facility. No matter how well you did, resist the temptation to jump for joy or call your significant other from the parking lot.

Different Types of Interviews

Now that we have covered the behavioral interview, you need to learn a little about some other interview types that you might encounter. This list is by no means all-inclusive, as new trends in interviewing are popping up daily. However, with a firm mastery on behavioral interviewing and a good understanding of these other interview formats, you will be set to win the interview.

Problem-Solving

Why is a manhole cover round?

How many quarters would it take to stack up as high as the Washington Monument?

You might be asking, "Are you serious?" Yes—these are real interview questions. This style of interviewing seems to be getting quite popular in the advent of Google and Microsoft trying to see who will come up with the most clever question each year.

When answering problem-solving questions, you must address the thought process involved in dealing with the issue, as well as the solution or answer you propose. The interviewer is more concerned with seeing how you tackle complex problems than he or she is with your specific answer. Much like the SOAR Method, I have developed have a simple way for you to remember how to go about answering these questions. Just remember that problem-solving is usually done in CLASS.

C	**Consider the constraints and limitations.**
L	**Listen to the entire question.**
A	**Ask for details.**
S	**Support your thought process.**
S	**Summarize your idea or solution.**

Why is a manhole cover round?

Before you go spouting off one of the most common answers, be sure you remember to apply the CLASS method to share your reasoning. Here are some of the most common responses:

- ➲ Because manholes are round!

- ➲ A round manhole cannot fall through itself. Conversely, if a square cover were placed diagonally across a square opening, it would fall through the hole.

- ➲ The tube it covers is round because the circular shape offers the best compression ratio possible to the underground pressure.

- ➲ When placing, they do not need to be rotated or orientated in any particular direction, which could be a problem because of their weight.

- ➲ More easily moved by being rolled.

- ➲ Tradition.

- ➲ Supply and Demand—where would you buy a square one?

Here is how you would apply the CLASS method to respond.

C: Well, as I am sure you know not all manhole covers are round.

L: In fact, some countries use triangles to indicate water flow direction.

A: I am sure you are asking about the majority of manhole covers here in the United States, right?

S: I think that that when manhole covers were first introduced to our country, they were most likely delivered to various staging points during construction and then rolled into place manually.

S: So, I believe that manhole covers are round due to a combination of ease of movement and tradition.

How many quarters would it take to stack up as high as the Washington Monument?

If you are like most people, you are now wishing that you had paid attention in your high school trigonometry class. But you don't need to worry about that if you use the CLASS method! Now if you happen to know off the top of your head that the Washington Monument stands 555 feet tall, then you will really impress the interviewer with your trivia knowledge. But even if you don't, all you have to do is apply the CLASS method to walk him or her through your logic.

For the following example, let's assume you did not know the exact height of the structure.

C: Well, because I do not have the actual dimensions for a quarter or for the monument, I am going to have to make some assumptions.

L: If I understand you correctly, you want to know how many quarters it would take to equal the height of the Washington Monument, right?

A: Are you referring to the Washington Monument on the mall in Washington, D.C. or the original Washington Monument in Baltimore?

➲ When you say "as high as the monument", do you mean above sea-level or above ground?

➲ Does it matter if the quarters are stacked end to end or one on top of the other?

S: By estimating that the average diameter of a quarter is approximately 1 inch and estimating that the monument is 600 feet tall, I would then use a simple calculation to reach a conclusion: 600 x 12 = 7,200

S: Therefore, I think it would take 7,200 quarters stacked end-to-end to equal the height of the Washington Monument.

As you can see in these examples, it is the process that is more important. The interviewers want to observe your cognitive skills in action and under pressure.

Telephone

Many interview processes start off with a phone interview. Phone interviews are even harder to demonstrate your skills and abilities than face-to-face interviews because the interviewer cannot see your enthusiasm or read your body language. They can, however, pick up on several clues that might prevent you from getting the face-to-face. I have yet another acronym for you to remember—IMPRESS. Just remember that you want to IMPRESS the interviewer to get to the face to face.

I	Inquire
M	Minimize Distractions
P	Phone Settings
R	Resources Up
E	Enthusiasm
S	Stand Up
S	Smile

Inquire

Always start off a phone interview by asking the other party if you have a good connection and be sure they can hear you clearly.

Minimize Distractions

Most people conduct phone interviews from home or work, if they have a private office. The one thing you should never do is a phone interview in a place where outside noise or calls for your attention could distract you. Make sure you are in a quiet room with the speakers on your computer muted and your other devices (phones, intercom, and so on) turned off.

• • •

I once had a candidate conduct an interview for a position with a marketing company where he would be working from his home office the majority of the time. I briefed him on the IMPRESS method and made sure he was fully prepared for the interview. About 15 minutes after his scheduled interview time, the hiring manager called me to ask why I had wasted his time with someone that clearly was not able to handle the work/life balance needed to function out of a home office. As it turns out, five minutes into the interview, the candidate's 2-year-old daughter came running into his office screaming for her daddy.

•

Phone Settings

Never use a mobile phone for a phone interview unless it is your only option. Even then, make sure it is plugged in to a charger and you are in a location with full reception. If you have call waiting, you should temporarily disable the service. For those of you that use a headset, make sure it has a full charge and you are within range.

Resources Up

One of the best things about a phone interview is that you can have your computer up and running as you speak. This can be especially helpful when referencing your accomplishments on your resume, if you need to do some quick research on the company, or if you need to refer back to your matrix of SOAR stories for your responses.

Enthusiasm

Make it a point to be overly enthusiastic when on the phone. Your impact presence cannot be seen so it is okay to be a bit more enthusiastic than you normally would be in person.

Stand Up

Get up out of your chair and walk around. This is when a wireless headset comes in handy. Your voice projects better when you are standing, and your energy level can be felt through the phone.

Smile

Look at yourself in the mirror and force yourself to smile. Much like standing and walking around, your energy level and enthusiasm are much more evident when you smile.

You must also remember to close using one of the techniques from Chapter 3.

Video Conference

With all the communication tools available today, some companies are reducing their travel expenses by conducting some or all of their interviews over video conferencing. Some use a professional service that they will ask you to join for free to gain access, while smaller companies may use other free tools like Skype to interact.

Aside from the reduced travel expenses, companies are trending more in this direction for some other reasons. First, they can complete the interview process faster by not scheduling the next interview weeks in advance to capitalize on lower airfare. Companies also like the fact that some of the tools allow them to record the interviews as a data file to protect themselves against any potential liability, coach the interviewers on better techniques, and allow several managers to review a standard set of responses from one question and answer session.

There are even a few third-party recruiting companies attempting to make an entry into the market by recording your responses to a standard set of questions and then allowing them to be searched by recruiters or companies looking for candidates.

From the job seeker's perspective, the process can seem impersonal and even robotic, depending on the level of technology used. Remember to apply the same body language tips and tricks we discussed earlier and think of the camera as your point of reference for eye contact. Try to look directly at the recording device and resist the urge to look at the feed of the interviewer on your monitor.

Many of the same tips discussed for phone interviews apply when preparing for a video conference interview, including minimizing your distractions, turning off your phone, a high level of enthusiasm, and smiling often. You should also ensure that your visible area (desk, table, and so on) is clean, professional, and free of clutter. If you are in doubt, then just remove any pictures from you wall and use a blank backdrop. Attire for a video interview is the same as if you were there in person, so assume business professional dress, unless told otherwise in advance.

• • •

I had a candidate that was interviewing for a Vice President of Sales position for a Fortune 500 national service business. It was a very high profile position and the interview process was very lengthy. The candidate lived in Southern California and the company's headquarters was in the Southeast. He had already made two cross-country trips to meet with members of the executive team, but was still unable to connect with one of the key decision-makers in the hiring process. The company suggested setting up a video conference for the two to connect as the final step in the process. It was almost a sure thing, as every person that he had met previously was eager to get him on the team. The interview was being administered by a third-party service that had a location near the candidate's home where he was to conduct the video interview. The candidate nailed the interview. At the end of the session, however, with the camera and audio still live; he stood up and revealed that he was wearing shorts under his coat and tie. He then proceeded to announce to the technician administering the session that he hated wearing a suit and tie and that it was a good thing he would be working remotely so his new company would never know! Of course the interviewer on the other end saw and heard it all. No offer was presented because of this lack of judgment.

•

Social

Social interviews are a very common tool companies use to see how you act in an informal setting. Do not mistake the social interview as a break from the process or as a free meal. You are still being evaluated. Doing well on a social interview may not win you the job, but doing poorly will certainly lose you the opportunity. These interviews mostly occur over a meal, but can sometimes be held at a trade show, convention, or business networking event. Companies hold social interviews for two reasons.

The first is to get to know you in a more informal way to determine if you are really a good fit with the culture of the team. This is especially common when you might be interviewing for a team-based position. In these instances, the social interview is usually near the end of the process once they have already determined that you can do the tasks required, but they just need the confirmation that your interaction skills will make you a productive member of the team.

The second purpose is to see how you perform in a social setting if part of your duties requires you to interact with customers or prospects in public. The interviewer(s) wants to see how you engage with those outside your previously established comfort zone and assess your etiquette, social grace, and manners.

Here are a few pointers for your next social interview:

Meals

- Order conservatively, even if you are at a fine dining restaurant. It is okay to order a nice meal, but just do not go over the top. For example, if the interviewer takes you to The Palm steakhouse, go ahead and get a steak, but hold off on the surf and turf combo with the five-pound lobster.

- Be polite and courteous to the host and wait staff.

- Try not to order anything that requires you to use your fingers or hands.

- Use good table manners.

- Wait until everyone is served before you begin eating.

- Set your knife and fork down after every bite.

- Place your napkin in your lap.

- Offer to pay for your meal—they will never let you, but it shows gratitude.

- Thank everyone present from the company for the meal.

• • •

My team and I were interviewing a candidate to come work for us as a recruiter. After a full morning of interviews, we all felt pretty good about him and signaled to each other that he was a candidate worth continuing the interview process with by taking him out to lunch. The candidate let his guard down and began a downward spiral that was unrecoverable. Not only did he order ribs and proceed to lick his fingers, completely disregarding his napkin; he also ordered a beer with lunch after we had all ordered iced tea. I was disgusted watching him chew with his mouth open and was thankful we had this social interview, or else we would all have been stuck with these horrible manners on a daily basis.

•

Drinks

- Only order an alcoholic drink if your company does so first.

- Limit yourself to no more than two drinks.

Networking Events

- If you meet people from outside the company you are interviewing with, be sure you tell your interviewers how you met them and what you discussed.

- Collect business cards from everyone with whom you speak.

- If invited ahead of time, ask about the attire.

Rides Alongs and Tours

Ride alongs and plant tours are very common steps in the interview process. Ride alongs are most common for outside sales and route sales positions. Plant tours are for production, manufacturing, distribution, and engineering positions, to name a few. Just like social interviews, you must remember that you are still being evaluated when on these types of interviews. Field rides and tours are a more relaxed setting, but they are still interviews.

For both types, be sure you bring a notepad with you. In most instances, you will debrief with the hiring manager or HR at the end of the day. They will ask what you thought, and you can then easily refer to your notes to offer specific events you encountered. It is much more professional than saying the typical response of "… it was great, exactly what I thought it would be." Rather, list some detailed items that you encountered and close again.

Ride Alongs

The most common types are for outside sales or route sales positions. You should know going in that the company is not just sticking you with any rep or driver; it is most likely pairing you up with one of its top people. The person with whom you are riding typically has to fill out a feedback sheet on you at the end of the day that finds its way back to your application packet. So if you see him or her taking notes on you, don't worry—it is part of the process.

The main reason people do *not* move forward after a ride along is because of too many outside distractions—most commonly too many phone calls. Your best bet is to leave your phone at home or in your car, but it is okay to take it with you in case of emergencies. If you do take it with you, set it to go directly to voice mail, and put it on vibrate or silent.

• • •

Last year I had a candidate interviewing for an outside sales position with a tool company. He was on a ride along with a rep from the company visiting some of the local Home Depots and Lowe's where their product was distributed. Not only did he take his phone with him against my instructions; but he proceeded to conduct a phone interview with another company while in the car with the rep. The rep dropped the candidate off at his car and terminated the field ride early. I commend the rep for not wasting any more of his time with a candidate who could not even provide him with the courtesy of his undivided attention for a few hours.

•

Tips for Ride Alongs

- Ask the rep how you should introduce yourself throughout the day. Some will say you are in training while others will want you to say that you are on an interview. Whatever they suggest is what you should go with.

- Introduce yourself to the contacts or prospects.

- Get involved in the sales calls to a point. Just keep your interaction to general business questions like "How is business?" but leave the technical or industry-specific topics to the rep.

- For route sales positions, be sure you pitch in and carry some of the load. If you don't get your hands dirty, then you will not be asked back.

- Ask questions about:

  ⮞ Competitors: Who is the strongest in this particular market? How do you sell against them?

  ⮞ Challenges: What would they have liked to know starting out that they know now? Was the training sufficient? How about support materials—proposals? Marketing sheets?

  ⮞ Opportunities: How is the current market? Is the prospect database big enough to support meeting President's Club (or whatever it is called there)?

  ⮞ Culture: How are field sales reps supported? Is it a fun place to work?

Plant or Facility Tours

When you conduct a plant or facility tour, you are usually escorted by one of your interviewers. The purpose is to not only show you where you will be working, but also to see how you interact with the people in the facility.

Tips for Plant Tours

- Interact with the people you meet throughout the tour. Tell them why you are there and shake hands. Ask them questions about their specific work station or area of responsibility.

- Thank each person you meet for his or her time and compliment each person in some way like "...thank you for sharing that with me. It looks like you do an awesome job here and I hope to see you again soon."

- Ask questions about:

  ⮕ Process: Who designed the process? Is this standard throughout your company or industry?

  ⮕ Equipment: How are preventative maintenance cycles conducted? What are the safety protocols associated with this piece of machinery? What is the through-put?

  ⮕ Environment: How do the employees feel about the facility? What are the most common employee concerns?

Panel

A panel interview consists of two or more interviewers in a setting typically meant to challenge the candidate to see how he or she performs under pressure. Panels are usually made up of an assortment of departmental managers and a representative from human resources or talent acquisition. Most panel members have a role that they assume either naturally or as a supporting character type to balance out the panel dynamics. You should know this going in and expect to encounter the following roles.

The Intimidator

This person will be easily identified because he or she will be the negative influence in the group. When dealing with the intimidator, be sure you look him or her squarely in the eye and smile as you respond to each of his or her questions. In some instances, the intimidator may make comments to other panel members without asking for your opinion. In these rare instances simply ask, "Can I clarify that for you?", "Did that answer your question sufficiently?", or "Would you like me to further elaborate?" At all costs, avoid getting into an argument with the intimidator. If you do, then you have lost.

If the intimidator is so negative that you feel harassed or insulted, you should stand, address the panel and state, "I'm sorry, but I was under the impression that this was a professional interview. Obviously not all members of the panel feel the same way and I would like to excuse myself. Should you like to meet again under more professional circumstances, you have my contact information." Any company that would expose you to insults and harassment is no place you want to work anyway, so just bow out with dignity.

The Coach

The coach is your guide to success. He or she will act as your champion and tell other panel members about your successes. Your coach is usually the person that you have been dealing with to set up the interviews.

The Observer

This is the person who is hard to read and may not even speak throughout the entire panel. You should never neglect the observer and include him or her when you make eye contact during your responses to questions, from other panel members. Try to engage the observer in the conversation by asking him or her a question if afforded the opportunity.

Tips for Panel Interviews

When you enter the room, greet every member of the team. If introductions are made, be sure you jot down their names or quickly commit them to memory. If none are offered, simply introduce yourself and wait to be asked to take your seat.

When answering questions from panel members, always look the questioner in the eye and begin your SOAR story. As you relay your response, gradually shift your eye contact to each member of the panel and return to the questioner to finish your response.

If you are interrupted while giving an answer by another panel member, stay calm and acknowledge the question or comment by stating "Good question/comment, but before I reply, I would just like to add to my response from the previous question that..."

When exiting, if at all possible, shake hands with each panel member and collect a business card from each. You will need this as part of your follow-up responsibilities.

Presentations

Another type of interview you might encounter is the presentation interview. In this format, you are tasked with a sales presentation of a course of action to an audience. In this setting, you are being judged on your interpersonal skills, presentation abilities, and ability to generate buy-in for your topic. As with any presentation, you should spend 80 percent of your time preparing and rehearsing and 20 percent of your time executing.

Most companies will give you a clear set of instructions or guidelines on your topic as well as the limitations (number of slides, time allowed, and so on) well in advance. If not, it is perfectly acceptable to ask for some guidance, and even ask if you could view previously presented materials as a baseline. As always, ask about attire before you show up.

The following outline should help you formulate your presentation topic:

Develop

Topic

If you have to come up with a topic on your own to sell the audience something, stick with what you know. If you like to run, then sell them on your brand of running shoe. If you like football, then sell them on the Sunday Ticket satellite package. If you are given a topic, make sure you dig deep in your research. If you have to pull information to support your topic, make sure you use at least three different sources, and have a bibliography handy in case it is asked for by the panel or audience.

Guidelines

Stick to the playbook. Do not exceed the recommended number of slides because you want to impress the audience with your research prowess. Part of the exercise is to see how well you follow directions and to see if you can concisely relay the highlights of an in-depth topic.

Create

Outline

Use these guidelines and do not try to cram too much material into any category.

- Introduction—10 percent of material and slides. State what it is you are trying to accomplish.

- Body—80 percent of material and slides. Use the 3Cs method.

- **Convey** the features and benefits.

    ⮎ Feature—A factual uniqueness about the product or service.

- ⊃ Benefit—A perceived need stemming from a stated feature.

- ⊃ "This phone has Push to Talk." (Feature)

- ⊃ "It allows you to connect without waiting for the other party to answer." (Benefit)

- **Cite** references from credible sources.

  - ⊃ "According to a recent article published by…"

  - ⊃ "As quoted in the *Journal of…*"

- **Cover** referrals from well-known personalities.

  - ⊃ "I use this service because…"
    —Expert Name

  - ⊃ "This product has changed the way…"
    —Celebrity Name

- Closing—10 percent of materials and slides. Always check for understanding by asking, "Are there any questions concerning the materials covered?" Then close by asking each member of the audience if he or she would like to buy!

Slide Rules

- Font Size—Assume that your audience is blind. Use a big font that can be read from across the room.

- Bullets—No more than three bullets per page.

- Animation—Leave it for the PowerPoint geeks. While a bullet that flies onto the screen with the sound of a jet engine might be cool to you, it is not going to score you any points in a professional presentation.

- Rehearse—If I have not already beaten the rehearsal horse to death, we will now. Practice and then practice some more.

- Video Yourself—Look at your posture and positioning.

- Never reach across your body to point at a bullet on the slide.

- Don't stand in front of the projected image.

- Keep focused on your audience and speak to them, not at the slides.

- Time Yourself—Stay within the time allotted, and make sure your speech pattern is not too fast. If you are not given a time in your guidelines, be sure you ask before you begin so you will not get cut off due to constraints.

- Deliver—Confidently cover your materials or pitch. Ask for questions at the end and always close.

Tests & Assessments

Many employers use tests or assessment profiles as part of the interview process. These tools are used to screen applicants in a number of different ways for a particular position. While there are many different types of tests and assessments, most will fall into one of five main categories: cognitive, skill assessment, personality profile, physical ability, and simulation.

Most employment candidates cringe when they hear the words "pre-employment testing" or "personality dynamics profile". It is true that testing in any form can cause stress for some people, but we all must realize that pre-employment testing and assessments are not designed to eliminate you from the process. Rather, they are tools interviewers use to see how closely you fit their concept of an ideal fit. It is imperative to remember to keep a positive outlook during this segment of the interview process. If tests make you nervous, do not show it to the interviewer.

Contrary to some beliefs, employers do not use testing to harass potential employment candidates or to find ways around diversity guidelines. Testing is a big expense for most companies. Some tests can run as much as $2,000 each, and full-simulation exercises can run more than $10,000, not to mention the time involved with administering them. Some tests that are used by employers are loosely regulated by a host of different state and federal agencies. However, the majority of testing is a private enterprise with varying degrees of validity and application. Validity refers to how a test measures the desired results. Most cognitive tests have undergone extensive validity studies by trained professionals. When the government does get involved is if a candidate feels a test was discriminatory. They will look at how the test was applied and determine if it was it given to all candidates for the position, if it was given at the same point in the process, how it was administered, and so on.

You are by no means required to take a test. However, you should know that by refusing to take the test that you will most likely be exited from the process. Some job-seekers just do not want to take tests. If you feel that way, then make sure you ask the recruiter or human resources representative early on what the specific steps in the interview process are so you do not waste either party's time.

Cognitive Tests

Most people know this type of test by their more common names: Intelligence Tests, IQ Tests, or Logic Tests. The content of these tests is made up of math problems, word associations, logic patterns, and the like. These types of tests were very common a decade or two ago, but have since lost popularity. The reason for their decline is due to the fact that some demographics or classes of the population have been proven to consistently test out lower than other socio-economic groups. As a result, there have been numerous lawsuits and discrimination claims against companies that solely use cognitive testing as a pre-employment screening tool. In today's market, you typically see cognitive tests used in conjunction with a personality profile or even included as a segment within a personality profile.

Specific Skill Assessments

This type of test is often seen for more technical positions. Engineers, coders, and technicians typically see skill assessments as part of the employment process before even getting a face-to-face interview. While some companies use their own internally developed skill assessments, most employers rely on industry accepted products that cover their area of expertise. If you are facing a skill assessment, always ask for the name of the test in advance and on which topics you should focus your study efforts. Some employers may even offer a study guide, but some simple web research will yield you a ton of sample tests and study materials if you know the name of the test.

Personality Profiles

These tests are quite common for sales representatives and mid- to upper-level management candidates. They may be administered in person, but the trend has been moving towards taking them online from the comfort of your home or office. Some are very short (20 minutes) and some are quite long (1 to 4 hours self paced). There are so many on the market and all vary slightly, so it is nearly impossible to mention the nuances between them all. However, the most common ones are Caliper, Gallup, Myers-Briggs, and DISC.

The important thing you need to remember when taking a personality profile is to answer honestly and go with your first impulse. Your results will not be accurate if you try to outsmart the test and provide answers you think the employer will want to hear. Remember, your results are being measured against a benchmark of the ideal profile for a particular position. Typically, companies will administer the very same assessment to their top-performing individuals in the targeted role and map your responses against theirs. I have taken all the tests previously mentioned, and they all came back with a very similar description of my leadership style. Just be yourself and do not try to trick the test. The worst thing that can happen will be that the interviewer will now have a set of questions developed from the profile for his or her next line of questioning. Think of these as objections and use the ECIR and SOAR Methods to overcome the objections.

If presented with some "challenges" or "concerns" with your profile, do not get argumentative or blame the test. For example, if your profile comes back as lacking thoroughness and the interviewer brings this up you could reply by saying, "I can understand why the results might show that. I believe that I am a very focused person, have a high level of attention to detail, and always follow through on tasks. However, I am willing to sacrifice some less impactful details for the sake of mission accomplishment. Is there a specific situation in this position where this might apply?" You have now turned the table and asked the interviewer to show you when in this position thoroughness is important. You have also deflected the objection without arguing or showing your frustration towards the test.

Physical Ability

Physical Ability tests are most common when you are applying for positions that involve some type of activity that could be potentially harmful or hazardous if you are not physically capable of performing the tasks associated with the job. The most common abilities measured are strength, speed of motion, and balance. These tests are most commonly administered by a physician's office and are not meant to be discriminatory towards people with disabilities. These tests typically involve a series of stretches, grip tension analysis, and lifting of an object similar in weight and dimensions as you would encounter in the workplace. These tests are used is to help employers minimize risk (such as worker's compensation insurance claims) due to the most likely injuries in that particular work place that result in someone not being able to perform his or her assigned duties. The most prevalent injuries employers see that lead to lost time are muscle sprains and strains, and repetitive strain injury (RSI), the most common form of which is Carpal Tunnel Syndrome.

Simulations

The final type of test or assessment you might encounter is a simulation. Some employers will refer to this as a role-play scenario, or for more senior executives, you might hear it referred to as an in-basket exercise. Whatever the case, it is a situationally based exercise to see how you interact (with peers, subordinates, and superiors), delegate, handle stress, and prioritize. Often, you will be presented with a study pack or some type of preparatory materials in advance of the exercise itself. Review the materials thoroughly and outline how you think the assessment will flow. The most common tasks assigned during these exercises include:

- Draft a letter to a client or customer (typically in response to a complaint).

- Develop an outline for a meeting in which you have limited time to cover numerous topics. Remember that you are expected to delegate some tasks, so go ahead and assign work to your virtual team and impose deadlines for deliverables.

- Counsel a subordinate on a violation of the employment policy. Typical situations include inappropriate dress in the workplace or using company resources for personal gain.

- Counsel a subordinate for failing to meet expectations. This is common for a sales leadership position in which you will role play against a poorly performing sales representative.

The most common challenge job seekers face with these types of tests is that they fail to use the latitude given to them. Not only is it acceptable, it is expected for you to make some assumptions and steer the assessment in the direction your judgment deems best. Most simulations will come with a debriefing period at the end in which you will be give the opportunity to explain why you chose a particular course of action. Stand by your actions and explain the reasoning behind your decisions.

There is still one more final set of pre-employment screening evaluations you are likely to encounter—the background check, drug screening, and driving record check. Each of these screening tools offer the employer a clear view into your background and decision-making process.

Background Checks

We covered this a bit earlier under illegal questions, but a more detailed explanation is warranted. Employers are allowed to ask job seekers if they have ever been convicted of a felony or if they have had any DUI convictions. It is not legal for employers to ask job seekers if they have ever been arrested. Convictions are the key. Employers are not legally allowed to remove you from the process due to arrests, only convictions. Most job applications ask for this info and then your signature authorizing a records check. Most records checks look for convictions in the state in which you are applying, but some do dig deeper.

If you do have convictions, disclose them. You only look like you are hiding something when you fail to do so. Even if you have had a conviction expunged, it may still show up on the records check. The software used today is quite detailed. If you are uncertain if a past conviction or arrest will show up on your record, your best bet is to purchase a background test on yourself prior to starting your career search to see what shows up. There are countless retailers online that will return your results within 24 hours.

Drug Screening

Employers are legally within their rights to conduct drug and alcohol screening tests as requirements to employment. They do this to ensure their work environment is free from potential hazards by screening out high-risk employees from the start. Employers do have some restrictions—pre-screening or testing of applicants for drug usage can only be done if it is administered fairly and consistently and if it complies with federal and state laws. Laws do vary with some states requiring that employers only test applicants once they have been presented with a formal job offer and that the offer is contingent upon a successful drug screen. Additionally, all employers that test must have a documented drug testing policy that stipulates the testing criteria and they must provide written notice to all applicants prior to the administration of any test.

If you are given a drug screen as a condition of employment, make sure you remember to list every over-the-counter medication and prescription drug you are taking on the test questionnaire, as they may show up on the test results. Employers cannot use this data to eliminate you from employment if you disclose it and are taking it legally as prescribed by a licensed physician. The most common drug tests look for marijuana, cocaine, opiates (Oxycontin, heroin, codeine) and amphetamines (Adderall, Dexedrine, Ritalin, Benzedrine), variations of which are commonly referred to on the street as Speed or Meth.

If a test returns a positive result, most labs will run more detailed testing prior to reporting back to the employer. These tests are very thorough and you cannot "beat" them by drinking large amounts of water, as many people believe. If you believe there was an error, you can always ask for a retest, but employers are under no obligation to comply. Be warned: alcohol will also show up in blood and urine tests even if you have one drink within 24 hours of the test, so be sure to disclose that in your questionnaire, but it is always best to refrain entirely before any testing.

Driving Record Check

If the position to which you are applying requires you to drive your vehicle or a company vehicle during the course of your duties, then the employer has the right to ask you questions about your driving record and even submit to a check of your record. Similar to background checks, these typically only return results for one state, but some are more inclusive. Everyone gets a speeding ticket at some point in their lives, so just disclose any moving violations up front.

CHAPTER 5

• • • • •

Follow Up

The actions you take after the actual interview are just as important as what you say during the interview. Your responsiveness, flexibility, and "get it done" attitude make a huge impact on your potential for an offer.

A great statement to open this type of inquiry call would be, "I am very excited about moving forward in the process and wanted to inquire as to the status of my last interview." *or* you could simply ask, "Where do we stand in the process?" It is perfectly acceptable to let your coach or contact know that you have other opportunities as long as you do not make it sound like you are forcing them to move faster than their normal process. In this case you might say, "I am very eager to complete the interview process with [company name] as it is one of my leading opportunities. I do have two other interviews that are at the offer stage and would like to be able to make an informed decision. When do you anticipate we will be able to complete the interview process so I can plan accordingly?"

If the process seems to be taking longer that you would like, it is perfectly acceptable to make a call to your coach, the contact you made that seemed to have driven the process the most, to check on status. What you should not do is go into "stalker mode" and call every hour to see where your offer is and when you will be starting. A good rule of thumb is that if you have not heard anything for two business days after your final interview, you can make the call. If more than a week goes by, unless you had previously been told the decision making timeline, you can call again. Remain professional at all times, even in the face of adversity.

Thank-You Notes

It seems that in today's society, many people have abandoned thank-you notes. This is a huge mistake that could cost you the position. Not only should you send a thank-you note, but you should send one to each person you met at each stage of the interview process. I know of several human resources professionals and hiring managers that will not even begin the information exchange within their company on a candidate until after a thank-you note is received.

Types

E-mail

While e-mail is a convenient method to communicate it is not the preferred method for thank-you notes. It is acceptable to use, however, only if you have previously established communications with the interviewer via e-mail. Your first e-mail to the interviewer should not be a thank-you note for the simple reason that it might go into his or her spam folder and never read. A good reason that you would use e-mail would be when you met with several people all on one day and you wanted to get a quick note to all of them as a group. If this is the case then include them all in the "To:" line.

Social Networking

It is becoming more and more prevalent to communicate via some form of social networking site for thank-you notes as well. Similar to e-mail, you should only use this method of delivery if you had previously established a connection on the social networking platform with the intended recipient. As always, when using social networking sites, be cautious as to who else might be privy to the post or communication you are sending.

Typed

Most interviewers perceive thank-you notes generated by a computer as impersonal. However, this format is fine to use, especially if you want to make use of the spell and grammar checking functions built into the software. Remember to also run your envelope through the printer, because nothing looks worse than a sloppy envelope with a typed letter.

Hand-Written

This is the preferred method for thank-you notes. By taking the time to write out your thoughts, you are showing the interviewer that you really care and that you put time into your actions. I suggest you use a blank card, or if you have personal stationery, that is also good. Don't spend hours in the card aisle looking for something to capture the moment. Stick with the basics.

Content

Personal

Each person you met with should get his or her own thank-you note, if possible. Make sure you reference a specific topic you discussed during the interview to show that that you were paying attention and that it made an impression on you.

Example Letters

Sales

Bill,

Thank you so much for taking the time to meet with me yesterday to discuss the Account Manager position. I am extremely excited about this opportunity and am eager to take the next step, which you mentioned was a ride along. Your explanation of the sales process and our local competition was helpful in gaining an understanding of the local market conditions. I look forward to seeing you again soon and joining your team.

Sincerely,

Dana Smith

Operations

Bill,

I sincerely appreciate the opportunity to interview for the Operations Manager position yesterday. Meeting the team on the plant tour and hearing their commitment and enthusiasm has convinced me that Wunder Widgets is a once-in-a-lifetime career opportunity that I would love to be a part of. I look forward to hearing from you again soon and am available for additional interviews at your convenience.

Thanks again,

William Chase

Timely

Postmarked within two business days of each interview.

Concise

No more than two paragraphs.

Check Spelling

If you are hand-writing a note, but are unsure about your spelling abilities, draft your letter on the computer first and then copy by hand with the correct spelling.

No Questions

The thank-you note is not a forum for interrogatives. Keep it to a simple thank you, a personal reference, and then a closing statement.

Communications

One of the most critical components during the follow-up phase is your availability. In today's fast paced and highly mobile world, your timely responses tell the tale of your interest level. The old adage of "If you snooze, you lose" is very accurate. Candidates that do not promptly reply to requests for documentation, references, or additional interviews are passed up for other more responsive candidates. The following list consists of some of the tips to help prepare you to be responsive and professional when communicating with a potential employer during this period.

Phones

As we mentioned previously, only use one phone number for contact purposes. Employers do not want to guess which number is best to reach you on. Make it an easy decision for them by giving them one solid contact number.

Consistency

Be sure your number will be active throughout your search. If you are relocating and are considering getting a local number, then make sure you get call forwarding on your old number until you secure your position.

Timely

Same-day callbacks are preferred. If the call to you was late in the day, then return it early the following day.

Notice

If your travel plans have you out of contact for any period of time during the follow-up period, then update your voice mail greeting to reflect such. It will let potential employers know in advance why you did not return their call promptly.

Voice mail Greetings

Listen to yours and ensure it is professional. State your full name and when you will return calls if you are traveling out of the area.

Personal

Use your voice to make a personal greeting. If your automated greeting just states your number, the employer might wonder if they reached the correct line or not.

No Music

Employers do not care who your favorite group or artist is. Similarly, do not use any ring back tones.

No Recordings

I know some of you use purchased or downloaded recordings for your greeting. Please remove them while you are searching for a new job.

Others

If you happen to share a phone with your significant other, or if you are using a shared land line, make absolutely certain that whomever might answer your phone is aware of your job search and which companies might be calling you. Keep a list by the phone, with you, and with your spouse.

The Turn Down

It is bound to happen to even the best of us for a myriad of reasons. You might have had an off day, the interviewer might not have liked your shoes, you may never know! Job interviews can be awkward beyond your control. It is how you handle the recovery that makes you stand out and look like a professional.

Professionalism

After hearing that you did not get the job, your communications with the company or interviewer are not necessarily over. While you may have experienced a minor setback, you should demonstrate to the company your professionalism and communication skills by composing a brief thank-you note for the time and opportunity. If you happen to know the exact reason for you removal from the process do *not* attempt to overcome it in a note to the interviewer; simply move on to the next opportunity.

• • •

I once had a candidate for a Director of Sales position with a Fortune 1,000 company. The candidate performed well in the interviews, but was ultimately not selected. The company told me that they wanted to keep him as a backup candidate in case their internal candidate did not work out. After hearing from me that he was not getting the offer and that the company went with an internal employee, he sent an e-mail to every person he interviewed with during the process. In that e-mail, he spoke negatively about their process and chastised them for taking up so much of his time. The client later told me that their internal candidate did not work out due to a relocation issue and that they would have moved on the other individual had he not acted so unprofessionally.

•

Look Ahead

It is important to do a quick self assessment on where you could have performed better in the interview, but don't over analyze to the point of second-guessing every single response or action. If you can't figure out where you were off, then just chalk it up to the interviewer's inability to see your potential. If you do know where your miscue lied (knowledge about the company or industry, lack of technological experience, and so on) make a point to adjust or address the potential objection before it comes out and rehearse for the next round of interviews. Remember the analogy we used about the professional golfers at the beginning of the book. Even those great professional golfers land one in the pond every now and then, but they shake it off and focus on the next shot.

Offers and Negotiations

Congratulations! You have made it to an offer. For some, this is the end of the road. For others, there is still some pavement in front of you left to be traveled. This final section will show you how to best traverse the final stretch once an offer has been presented.

The Offer

Offers come in many different forms and can be delivered either orally or in writing. I always recommend asking for the offer in writing, even if it has been delivered orally. Keep in mind that there may be some other factors going on behind the scenes that the person who gave you the offer verbally may not have control over. The main reason for these delays is because some companies require signatures from a higher department or authority within the company. As simple as it seems, sometimes this can take a few weeks, which is why the hiring managers like to get a verbal first before they stick their necks out to get a signature form their bosses.

What It Looks like

Most offers are fairly easy to read and provide details of all aspects of your employment. Some may be contingent upon a successful background check, drug screening, or driving record check if you will be operating a company vehicle.

Bonus and Commission Plans

If part of your overall compensation package includes any type of bonus, commission, or equity sharing, then make sure you get it in writing with the offer. All too often I hear stories of people who accept a position under the impression that their commission of bonus is calculated differently than how it was explained to them in the interview process. If it not attached or included with the offer just ask, "Could I please have a copy of the bonus/commission plan as well?" If they say no, you should be very leery.

Deadlines

Some offers will include a deadline for acceptance. If you need a deadline because you are looking at other opportunities and none is given, then be sure to set the employer's expectations by explaining you will need X days to make your decision and ask if that is acceptable. The employer will naturally want to know why and you should be honest by saying that this opportunity is still your number one choice, but you also have another offer to review before reaching your final decision. Some employers will tell you that you need to make your decision right then and there. They are within their right to do so, and you should be ready if you find yourself in this scenario.

The Counter

For those of you that find yourself in the position where your current employer tries to counter to keep you, take heed. Most employers only do this for self-serving interests— they have no one to cover the territory, the project, or shift. While the extra cash might sound attractive, are you really making the right choice? Just think back to why you started looking in the first place. I have seen dozens and dozens of candidates that end up taking the counter to stay put, only to find themselves back on the market again a few months later.

Benefits Sheet

If your position includes a benefits package, then get the complete benefit coverage descriptions and rates with the offer. The human resources rep or department typically has all this info, but most hiring managers forget to include it with the offer. The following lists some of the most common employment benefits and a brief explanation for each.

General Coverage

Find out if there are any monthly costs to enroll in the benefits plan and who is covered. Some plans have different rates for the employee and the family members. It should also spell out when coverage begins (start date or after a period of time). Lastly, ask about restriction on enrolling at a later date should you decline coverage initially, as some plans only allow for enrollments during certain periods.

Medical Insurance

There are entire volumes written on the different types of medical insurance, so just make sure you know the type of plan(s) available to you (typically PPO, HMO or HSA), what expenses are covered, deductible and copay rates, and any exclusions for pre-existing conditions. If all this sounds foreign to you, then sit down with the company benefits administrator or HR rep before you accept.

Dental Insurance

The most common questions are whether preventive care and orthodontic care are covered and to what extent.

Vision/Eye Care

This may be included in medical, but lately it is being listed as a separate benefit. Many companies now offer an "up to" amount of annual coverage, which can include exams, eyeglasses, and contact lenses.

Life Insurance

Though none of us like to think about it, this is a worthy investment and if your company has coverage, you should enroll. Most companies offer discount rates on term life insurance policies as long as you are employed there.

Accidental Death or Dismemberment

Some companies offer this in case you die on the job. If it is offered for free, then by all means take it. If not, then pass.

Disability Insurance

This is a benefit that most people elect not to receive and then kick themselves for not getting covered later. Disability insurance is usually divided into short-term disability and long-term disability. In short, it provides a percentage of your pay should be injured on the job and not able to work.

Vacation

The standard vacation policy may start with one to two weeks per year then additional days or weeks based on years of service. Most companies also pro-rate the first year based on the month in which you start. Ask whether vacation days accrue. Most do not, but if they do, then you can sell days back later for cash or take extended vacations in later years.

Holidays

There are 10 Federal holidays, but most employers only cover the "big six" which are: New Year's Day, Memorial Day, Independence Day, Labor Day, Thanksgiving Day, and Christmas Day.

Sick/Personal Days

Most small businesses do not have sick days, but larger companies still have policies for days off due to illness. Ask for the policy and make sure you understand it, as some sick days can go against your vacation days.

401(k) Plan

If the company has a 401(k) savings plan, you should enroll and contribute as much as you can early on, as the taxes associated with it are deferred until much later in life. Some companies also match your contributions (up to a certain amount). Ask what the match rate is and also ask what the vesting schedule is.

Profit Sharing

Profit sharing is when a certain percentage of the company's net income is spread out among its workforce. There are usually complex calculations involving tenure and salary rate to determine your individual allotment, but any amount is a good thing. This is a great benefit if offered because it forces the employees to remain focused on the company's overall success.

Stock Options

Options are usually only awarded with an offer for senior level positions. They are also used as awards for performance. Basically you are granted company stock that is held in escrow (the vesting period) until you are free to sell them. If the stock is then trading at a higher price, you get the difference. Beware of long vesting periods. Anything over four years to reach 100-percent vested may not be in your best interest, as the time it takes to reap the benefit might outlast your employment. These restrictions are rarely negotiable, as changes to one individual's options could be deemed preferential by other shareholders. The majority of plans I see are 25 x 4 (25-percent vested after year one, 50 percent after year two, and so on); 33 x 3 (33-percent vested after year one, 66 percent after year two, etc...); or Cliff Vesting at the third year (nothing until the end of the third year and then 100-percent vested all at once).

ESOPs

Employee Stock Ownership Plans allow you to buy company stock on a schedule at a rate less than the market price. Most companies require you use their broker to do this and may charge a nominal fee that comes right out of the set allotment. You benefit in the long run, as your stock is worth more than the average guy who bought the same number of shares at the same time you did.

Tuition Reimbursement

A nice benefit if you plan to pursue an advanced degree during your free time.

Gym Memberships

An emerging trend is to keep the workforce happy by offering full or discounted gym memberships to local establishments. Some are "use it or lose it" plans that require a minimum number of monthly visits to keep the benefit active.

Childcare

If offered, it can save you thousands of dollars a year. Some companies even have on-site childcare so you can continue to spend time with your kids while you are on your lunch break.

Employee Assistance Programs

EAPs are formal programs designed to help employees that need assistance with numerous tasks such as financial aid, tax return services, drug or alcohol counseling, or even psychological care.

Overtime

If you are in an hourly rate position, make sure you know the rates and restrictions associated with overtime.

General Expenses

Most companies will pay you for authorized direct business related charges that you incur during the discharge of your duties. These can include mobile phone, customer entertainment, fuel, postage and shipping, and so on. Know the policy and know what is covered. Don't try to submit expenses that are not directly related to the business, or you will find yourself starting the job search process all over again.

Negotiations

If you are negotiating, then you must really want the position. Do not waste the employer's time negotiating if you have no intention of accepting the position. Negotiations are not a crutch you can lean on as a reason for turning an offer down. You are better off just turning the offer down outright if that is your intent. Many candidates make the mistake of attempting to negotiate items that are non-negotiable and end up losing the opportunity. These candidates will insist upon items that they feel are competitive to their current situation, other offers, or their idea of what they should get; but in the end, the employer simply cannot adjust to meet their needs because it would mean changes to policy beyond their control.

So, let's first understand what is negotiable and what is not.

Negotiable	Non-Negotiable
Base Salary	Standard Benefit Rates
Annual Increase Rate	Overtime Rates
Annual Bonuses	Company Auto Rates
Signing Bonus	Expense Coverage
Stock Options	Profit Sharing
Relocation Expenses	
Vacation Time	
Commission Rates	

Even with all these possible areas of negotiation, most candidates focus on the salary. A general rule of thumb is that if the initial offer is within 10 percent of your desired salary then you should negotiate. Any difference greater than 10 percent and you are fighting an uphill battle.

• • •

A candidate we represented was presented an offer by an employer for a position that required a relocation. The candidate had already indicated that relocation was not a problem and that he understood the company had a policy prohibiting relocation expenses for this level position. When the offer was delivered, the candidate hesitated and explained to us that he was unable to accept unless the employer paid for the costs associated with moving his horse to the new city. As you can imagine, the employer was not about to pay for a horse relocation when they could not even pay for the new employee's relocation. We never presented the option to the employer in fear that they would revoke the offer altogether. After several long discussions with the candidate, we were successful in encouraging him to find a horse relocation carrier to move the animal at his own expense.

•

Pre-Close

The best way to prevent a salary negotiation is to set the employer's expectations before the offer is delivered. This way, the employer will know what it takes to get an immediate yes from you because the employer does not want to negotiate any more than you do.

Total Compensation vs. Salary

Remember all those benefits we just covered? Well they do have a value when you add them into your total compensation package. Often, candidates get a number stuck in their head that they feel they are worth and they might pass up an opportunity because they were shy of that number, when in actuality, the other position they end up taking has the number, but with a much lower benefit package, which ends up costing them more take home money that the lower salaried position with the good benefits.

Use Your Recruiter

If you have been working with a recruiter, then by all means use him or her to negotiate. Recruiters do it daily, and it prevents you from starting out your relationship with your new boss or employer on a sour note over a few thousand dollars.

Limitations

You must understand what you are up against. Most times, it is not the individual that you are negotiating against, but a policy that dictates a certain range for the position. If you find yourself in a negotiation that involves a range, the employer will tell you, and then you will need to get creative and look at other items to discuss.

Techniques

Here are proven techniques to assist when you find yourself close, but in need of a nudge to get to where you want to be.

- If You Could…Then I Would—This is a variant on a sales closing technique often used by salesmen to get the buyer to commit called "If I could _____, then would you_____?"

In this instance, you are telling the employer that you are ready to accept, if only he could make one small concession. "I am very interested in this position and the company; however, at this stage, I am not able to accept the offer because of the (salary, bonus, relocation package, and so on) If you were able to _____, I would gladly accept the position immediately."

In the blank above you could either say "...flex some on your end..." to keep it general, or you could list the specific desired outcome such as "...come up $3,000 on the base salary..." Either method works, it just depends on your confidence level.

- Almost There—"I just reviewed the offer and I think we are almost there. The offer is very close to where it needs to be for my immediate acceptance. Here is where we stand..." then add in the specific item or items that you would like to adjust. Close by asking them if they think these are fair adjustments.

- The Walk Away—If you feel you are at an impasse, then you have to be able to say "No thanks" and walk away. This is not a rejection, but more of a tactic if you feel they really want you. It occasionally works, but it does take a very high level of confidence to pull it off successfully. This technique should only be used if you have some inside knowledge that there is still some bargaining to be done and you feel that you are leaving money on the table. It is risky, so use it only when you are extremely confident of success.

- Rounds—Unlike a boxing match, you are not going to get 10 to 12 rounds of negotiations. Most negotiations regarding a job offer cover one round from each side. If a consensus has not been reached by then, the deal has minimal hopes for success. So, if you have multiple items for negotiation, don't hold one in reserve, let it all out and work up from there.

- Give and Take—Don't be demanding. A negotiation involves concessions made by each party to reach an agreeable middle road. We already covered how sometimes candidates get so focused on the salary number that they lose sight of the overall package. Employers may have restrictions due to policy that prevent salaries outside certain ranges and will attempt to cover the delta by providing signing bonuses or "stay" bonuses paid out after a predetermined period of time. The end result is that you earned the same amount, but just not in your salary. Be prepared to meet in the middle when you begin a negotiation.

Acceptance

When you are ready to accept, sign your offer letter and fax, scan and e-mail, or mail it back to your new employer. Always call upon acceptance and thank them for the opportunity. If you need to adjust your start date or need to keep it open, then just tell them. Some employers only start new hires on certain days to minimize their orientation expenses. If anything should delay your anticipated start day, be sure to call right away. If your start date is longer than two weeks out, you should call weekly to let them know you are still on track for your start date.

Rejection

If you do get to the point where you are going to reject an offer, do so with the utmost professionalism. You never know where the future leads and it is never good to burn a bridge behind you. Thank them for the offer and tell them that you have decided to pursue another opportunity. If they ask for details you can offer them up if you like, but in most cases, it is best to keep your reasons general in nature.

• • • • •

Review

Remember at the very beginning of the book when we discussed the two main things you will need to do to win the interview?

- Sharpen and finely tune your interviewing skills so that you will be in a position to win every interview.

- Make your career transition your number-one priority—no window shopping or testing the market.

By now you should have a very good grasp on the first item and you can further sharpen your skills by completing the worksheets that follow. By finishing this book and taking notes along the way, you have also committed yourself to making your career transition your number-one priority. Congratulations!

Remember, interviewing is a skill-based discipline. Even if you are the most qualified candidate, have the perfect resume, and possess the right background and career path for a particular opportunity; you may still lose the interview if your interviewing skills are not sharp. As with any skill-based discipline, the more you practice, the better you will perform. The tips, tricks, and techniques we covered are no substitute for your attitude, perseverance, and focus on your career search. Use them as tools to aid in your skill development and keep refining the skills.

Lastly, if all else fails during your next interview, remember these two things and you will do better than most of your peers.

- Tell SOAR stories when answering questions.

- Close—Even if you think the interview was a complete disaster, close using one of the methods we covered.

Sample Resumes and References

Chronological Resume

FIRST LAST

1234 Any Street
Anytown, US 12345
(321) 098-7654, name@isp.com

EXPERIENCE:

Service Company, Customer Service Team Lead (6/08 – Present)
Tampa, FL

Lead a 30-person customer service team in a call center
Tracked all key performance indicators for entire team
Interviewed and trained new customer service representatives
Was responsible for second level call response for entire floor
Provided daily and weekly reports to the Director of Customer Service
Participated in weekly staff meetings

- Reduced the shift's average Time to Resolution from 3:37 to 2:54
- Developed new call scripts for several reoccurring questions
- Team was ranked #1 of 4 in total customer satisfaction

Business Name, Customer Service Representative (7/06 – 6/08)
Atlanta, GA

Handled in-bound customer service calls for three different business lines in a call center setting. Dealt with billing and payment questions and assisted customers with accound management for cell phone accounts.

- Awarded CSR of the Month award 3 times in a 12-month period. Only multiple award redipient in the company
- Received 27 letters from satisfied clients referencing personal service provided

Chronological Resume (continued)

FIRST LAST
Page two

Business Name, Office Intern (9/05 – 6/06)
Washington, DC

Assisted Office Manager in various office functions including reception, accounts payable, accounts receivable, sales support, administrative support, and customer service. Attended staff meetings and presented weekly lessons learned to the Office Manager.

- Extended offer of full-time employment after graduation
- Recognized by the Office Manager as instrumental in the office's perfect audit score

EDUCATION:
BS Marketing – University of Maryland, 2006

- Chapter President, National Sorority
- Intramural soccer

ADDITIONAL INFORMATION:

- Enjoy running, reading business periodicals, and golf
- Graduate of Dale Carnegie training

Functional Resume

FIRST LAST
1234 Any Street
Anytown, US 12345
(321) 098-7654, name@isp.com

Summary of Qualifications

Highly motivated leader with eight years' corporate experience. Proven ability to motivate and work effectively with teams to produce results. Especially skilled at building effective, productive working relationships with customers via a consultative approach. A natural communicator with exceptional interpersonal ability, excellent written and verbal communication skills and a proven record of accomplishment. Mission-focused and results-driven performer, while never losing sight of the importance of people. Energetic self-starter with excellent analytical, organizational, and creative thinking skills. A talent for analyzing problems, developing and simplifying procedures, and finding innovative solutions. Committed to the highest levels of professional and personal excellence.

Selected Accomplishments

Leadership:
- Managed 46-person team, providing operations and maintenance in support of $18M worth of field-deployed medical diagnostic equipment.
- Named as head customer support contact for $70M merger integration effort. Acted as the single point of contact for application integration teams responsible for system merger of two Fortune 500 companies.

Functional Resume (continued)

FIRST LAST
Page two

Communications:
- Compliance Manager; Designed, promoted and taught six worldwide training seminars in person and through use of Web-based services.
- Presented equipment upgrade plan to division vice president; received $2.3M budget approval. Completed project under budget and ahead of schedule.

Initiative:
- Engineered equipment tracking system upgrade with RFID, ensuring visibility of all assets deployed through distribution center.
- Developed data solutions providing worldwide access to critical scheduled and preventative maintenance records for all devices.

Performance:
- Promoted from IT Manager to Division Director within 11 months of joining new company
- Star of Excellence Award finalist; Presented to #1 IT Professional in 350-person IT Department

Med Device Company	2002 – Present
IT Manager	2002-2003
Division Director	2003 - Present
IT Start Up Firm	201 - 2002

Education:
BS in Computer Engineering, ITT Tech – Palmdale, CA

- 4.0 GPA

Combination Resume

FIRST LAST

1234 Any Street

Anytown, US 12345

321) 098-7654, name@isp.com

Extensive background in managing all the aspects of an operational P&L to include sales, operations, logistics, customer service, and administration. Results-oriented in achieving quality, service, new markets, efficiencies and cost reduction goals/objectives. Ability to grasp new concepts and ideas quickly and develop innovative methods to meet objectives. Sent into many operations/departments as corporation lead person to turn around ailing results and rebuild management teams. Qualified and ready to continue executive level responsibilities.

SUMMARY OF QUALIFICATIONS

➤ Six Sigma Black Belt with progressive experience in operations, logistics, sales, and customer service

➤ Consistent results achieved, over time, relative to quality, service, efficiency and cost objectives

➤ Skilled manager, negotiator, communicator, and leader; inspiring work teams to excel

➤ Expert process, strategy, organization and problem-solving capability through creative and analytical capabilities

➤ Ability to generate "out of the box" ideas and concepts to break existing paradigms and improve operations

✧ Inventory Management Control	Talent Recognition & Development
✧ Vendor/Customer Negotiations	Continuous Process Improvement
✧ Cost Reduction & Avoidance	Profit & Loss Leadership
✧ Team Building & Leadership	Workflow Planning & Prioritization

Combination Resume (continued)

FIRST LAST
Page two

PROFESSIONAL EXPERIENCE

Company Name   **Aug 2008 - Present**

Assistant Group Vice President   Sep 07 - Present

Responsible to the Group Vice President for the day-to-day operation of a $224 million business to business services company with revenues in excess of $32 million. Act as a resource in operational matters for 18 General Managers. Providing direct, local support, on site, in all sales and profit functions. Travel 60% of the time.

- Recognized as the subject matter expert in strategies to improve profitability in Group locations
- Certified **Six Sigma Black Belt** responsible for completing corporately directed projects focusing on increasing sales and profit throughout the company

General Manager   Dec 03 - Sep 07

Responsible for growth, profit and customer satisfaction for a business to business services location with sales in excess of $12 million and profits in excess of $2.0 million. Led an organization that consisted of 141 employees, 10 department managers and 7 supervisors.

- Achieved continued growth of 21% and profit of 17% over previous two years. Only location in Group to achieve new business goals
- Recognized as the #1 General Manager in the Group in FY06

Production Manager   Aug 99 - Dec 03

Responsible for overseeing the operation of 5 production facilities including: management, customer satisfaction and cost control for the #1 group in the corporation.

- Reduced group's overall cost of goods to below 15% over 2 years saving 5% under industry standards or approximatelly $10 million per year

EDUCATION

BS in Business Administration, University of California at Los Angeles – 1998

- Specializing in Production and Operations Management
- Captain of water polo team

Curriculum Vitae

FIRST LAST

1234 Any Street

Anytown, US 12345

(321) 098-7654, name@isp.com

EDUCATION	JD MBA - **University of Michigan**	2008
	BS - **Harvard University**	
	Business Administration	2005
HONORS	National Marketing Foundation Fellow,	
	Harvard University	2005
	Phi Beta Kappa	2004
	Dean's List, University of Michigan	2006-8

AREAS OF Business planning and strategy. Start up and entrepreneurial

SPECIALIZATION Planning. Investor relations, angel investing, venture capital presentations and pitches. Business plan writing and review. Profit and Loss, income statement review, financial and Income statements.

INTERN EXPERIENCE Review of monthly and quarterly financial filings for private and public companies. Presentation of findings to executive staff and participation in group and divisional group meetings. Field benchmark information gathering to determine best practice solutions for widespread implementation.

AFFILIATIONS/ MEMBERSHIPS Future Business Leaders of America

Online Marketers Association

Ecommerce Focus group for Applied Technology

Engineering Associates of America

Society of Professional Project Management Professionals

Curriculum Vitae (continued)

FIRST LAST
Page two

SOFTWARE/	BizPlan Pro	Advanced
PROGRAMMING	PeachTree	Proficient
	QuickBooks	Proficient
	MindFlash	Expert
	MS Project	Expert
	MS Office Applications	Advanced
	C++	Advanced
	.net	Proficient
	Ruby on Rails	Learning
	Photoshop	Proficient

WORK/	GreenGas Propane	Internship	2004
INTERSHIP	JuLuTech	Paid Internship	2005
HISTORY	The Lansing Project	Research Incubation Team	2007

References

FIRST LAST

1234 Any Street, Hometown, ST 12345

(321) 098-7654, name@isp.com

PROFESSIONAL REFERENCES

Mr. Samuel Jackson, VP of Sales (Current Immediate Supervisor)

1234 Work Drive	Phone: (123) 456-7890
Box #4321	E-mail: first.last@isp.com
City, US 12345	

Excerpt from performance evaluation:

"Aggressive sales representative that constantly surpasses goals. Self-motivated performer that needs minimal supervision to achieve company and personal objectives. The best sales representative I have ever had the pleasure of working with."

Mr. Owen Wilson, Regional Sales Manager, ***Acme Company*** (Former Employer)

1234 Performance Street	Phone: (123) 456-7890
Suite #A1A	E-mail: first.last@isp.com
City, US 12345	

Copy of personal note on work anniversary:

"I cannot thank you enough for your contributions to our team. You have accomplished more in your first year of sales than most reps dream of in their careers. We are thrilled to have you. Keep up the good work and congratulations on President's Club!"

References (continued)

FIRST LAST
Page two

Col Vince Vaughn (Former Military Unit Commander)

1234 Military Drive   Phone: (123) 456-7890

Box #4321   E-mail: first.last@us.mil

Hometown, US 12345

Excerpt from fitness report:

"An asset to any team. Ability to grasp complex concepts and immediately put into action. Performs at a level above his current rank and billet. Understands the principals of effective leadership and the importance of its impact upon out entire unit's success. Uncapped developmental potential, ready to assume increased levels of responsibility."

PERSONAL REFERENCES

Mr. Wil Ferrell

President, Integrity Pumps (Family Friend)

1234 Main Street   Phone: (123) 456-7890

Hometown, US 12345   E-mail: name@isp.com

Mrs. Jessica Simpson

Principal, Oak Grove High School (Former High School Principal)

1234 Education Lane   Phone: (123) 456-7890

Hometown, US 12345   E-mail: name@isp.com

Mr. Vincent Chase

Sales Director, Big Bear Films (Former Employer - Internship)

1234 Hollywood Blvd   Phone: (123) 456-7890

Hometown, US 12345   E-mail: name@isp.com

Salary History

FIRST LAST

1234 Any Street, Hometown, ST 12345

(321) 098-7654, name@isp.com

SALARY HISTORY

Company Name

1234 Work Drive

Box #4321

City, US 12345

Job Title (Dates)

Starting Salary/Rate: **Amount** (Round to nearest whole number)

Ending Salary/Rate: **Amount** (Round to nearest whole number)

Bonus and Commission Earned:

Year: **Amount**

Year: **Amount**

Stock Options Earned:

Year: **Amount**

Year: **Amount**

Job Title #2 (Dates)

Starting Salary/Rate: **Amount** (Round to nearest whole number)

Ending Salary/Rate: **Amount** (Round to nearest whole number)

Company Name

1234 Work Drive

Box #4321

City, US 12345

Job Title (Dates)

Starting Salary/Rate: **Amount** (Round to nearest whole number)

Ending Salary/Rate: **Amount** (Round to nearest whole number)

Bonus and Commission Earned:

Year: **Amount**

Year: **Amount**

SOAR Method Worksheets

While you may encounter different versions of the following questions, these should provide you with a solid baseline to develop your SOAR stories. The list is by no means all-inclusive, it is meant to teach you how to prepare for the questions. For each question, give your SOAR response an easily remembered name to jog your memory, should you encounter the question in an interview. The worksheet is for you to use to script out your responses and then use while you rehearse. I recommend making flash cards for each response with the question on the front and the SOAR response on the back.

Sales

- Why Sales?

- Describe for me a typical sales cycle in your current position.

- Tell me about a situation where your contact person changed at a key account and what you did to adjust to the new contact.

- What percentage of your targets did you achieve?

- How many appointments did you typically have in a week?

- Give an example of when you had to change your approach to gain access to a prospect.

- Give an example of when you had to overcome an objection from a prospect.

- Tell me about one of the most time-consuming sales you ever made.

S	Situation		15–20 Seconds
O	Objective		15–30 Seconds
A	Action		1–2 Minutes
R	Result		10–20 Seconds

- What goals have you set for yourself this year? How are you progressing?

- Tell me about a sale that you did not get.

- Give me an example of when you had to make a presentation to a panel or group.

- What do you enjoy most about sales?

Operations/Leadership

- Describe your leadership style.

- Do you perceive a difference between a leader and a manager?

- How do you function in a team setting?

- What would your peers say about you as a leader?

- What are the three most important values you demonstrate as a leader?

- Tell me about a time when you had a direct report that was not meeting expectations.

- During your college experience, tell me about a time when you demonstrated your leadership ability.

- How do you keep each member of the team involved and motivated, while keeping morale high?

- What steps do you take to ensure that the work you delegate is successful?

- What is the biggest area you could improve upon from a professional and personal developmental perspective?

Customer Service

- Tell me about a time when you had to deal with an angry client.

- Define customer satisfaction.

- What do you see as being the greatest challenges today in the customer service industry?

- Why do you like dealing with customers?

- Can you tell me about a time when you did something extra for a customer?

- How many orders/calls do you currently deal with on an average day?

PM/Engineering

- Give me an example of how you used your leadership skills to help your project team meet a difficult challenge.

- What was the most stressful aspect of your last project and how did you deal with it?

- Tell me about a situation during a recent project when you had to adapt or change directions.

- Describe the most complex project you have managed from start to finish.

- How do you manage you vendors?

- How do you keep organized?

- Describe the most significant written technical report or presentation that you had to complete?

- Tell me about your greatest success in using the principles of logic to solve an engineering problem.

Reference Card

Answering Behavioral Questions

S	Situation	Briefly describes the background information necessary to relay your specific example • "For example…" • "Just last month…" • "I had a recent situation where…"	15–20 Seconds
O	Objective	Tells the corrective action to change the behavior, practice, or process • "My challenge was to…" • "I had a huge task in that…" • "My goal was to…"	15–30 Seconds
A	Action	Relays the steps that were implemented • "I initiated…" • "I decided to…" • "I developed…"	1–2 Minutes
R	Result	Clearly demonstrates the positive outcome • "As a result, …" • "At the end of the day/project…" • "At the conclusion of…"	10–20 Seconds

Phone Interviews

I	Inquire
M	Minimize Distractions
P	Phone Settings
R	Resources Up
E	Enthusiasm
S	Stand Up
S	Smile

Problem Solving Questions

C	**Consider the constraints and limitations.**
L	**Listen to the entire question.**
A	**Ask for details.**
S	**Support your thought process.**
S	**Summarize your idea or solution.**

Phases of the Interview

Rapport Building
- Introductions—Smile and firm handshake
- Relax—Demonstrate confidence

Background Information
- "Tell me about yourself" in 2–3 minutes
- Chronological: Intro—Body—Conclusion
- Key selling points

Confirming Requirements
- Geography and relocation
- Work type to determine a match to position
- Salary requirements in line with position

Behavioral Questions
- Use the SOAR Method

Questions for the Interviewer
- 5–7 written and prepared before going in
- NOT training, WIIFM, or public knowledge
- Use assumptive phrasing

Closing Questions and Methods
- Always close every step of the process

Closing Methods

Isolation	• "Is there anything we covered today that would prevent me from moving forward in the interview process?"
Set-Up	• Align your skills and behavior traits with the ones the interviewer deems most important.
Assumptive	• "I think we had a great meeting and I am already looking forward to making an impact on your team."
Subtle	• "What is the next step in the interview process I can expect and when would you anticipate that occurring?"
Direct	• "Do you think that I am a match for the opportunity?"

• • • • •

Index

• • • • •

About the Author

Brian Davis is a well respected independent consultant in the recruitment sector. Mr. Davis recently served as the Chief Executive Officer of Talent Alliance, Inc., a global recruitment firm with offices in the United States and China that covers staffing, executive placement, contingency and retained search, and recruitment technology platforms. Prior to his tenure at Talent Alliance, Mr. Davis was a founder and principal of Soar Consulting Inc., a leader in the military-to-civilian transition recruitment sector. Mr. Davis also held numerous positions with the Cintas Corporation, a NASDAQ-100 company that has been recognized as one of America's "Most Admired" and "Best Companies to Work For" by *Forbes* Magazine, and by *Selling Power* Magazine as one of the "Top Ten Sales Forces" in the country.

Mr. Davis is a skilled public speaker that has presented seminars to audiences into the hundreds and conducted numerous radio interviews discussing topics relating to the recruiting and staffing business, interview preparation skills, and job seeker resources. He has personally coached and trained thousands of candidates across numerous industries from entry level positions to senior executives. Mr. Davis is often called upon by industry experts and the press to comment on the current status of the recruiting industry, new recruitment technology, and emerging trends in the sector. He resides in Temecula, California with his wife and two children, and travels extensively to consult with clients and candidates.

**Other Helpful Career Guides
From Career Press:**

Work at Home Now
Christine Durst and Michael Haaren
EAN 978-1-60163-091-9

Finding a Job After 50
Jeanette Woodward
EAN 978-1-56414-894-0

Highly Effective Networking
Orville Pierson
EAN 978-1-60-163-050-6

The Parent's Guide to Family-Friendly Work
Lori K. Long
EAN 978-1-56414-944-2

Visit CareerPress.com for more information.
To order call 1-800-CAREER-1

**Other Helpful Career Guides
From Career Press:**

Top Notch Executive Interviews
Katharine Hansen
EAN 978-1-60163-084-1

Top Notch Executive Resumes
Katharine Hansen
EAN 978-1-56414-989-3

Carve Your Own Road
Jennifer and Joe Remling
EAN 978-1-60163-052-0

Competency-Based Resumes
Robin Kessler
EAN 978-1-56414-772-1

Visit CareerPress.com for more information.
To order call 1-800-CAREER-1